Mometrix
TEST PREPARATION

Louisiana

US History EOC Success Strategies

Dear Future Exam Success Story

First of all, **THANK YOU** for purchasing Mometrix study materials!

Second, congratulations! You are one of the few determined test-takers who are committed to doing whatever it takes to excel on your exam. **You have come to the right place.** We developed these study materials with one goal in mind: to deliver you the information you need in a format that's concise and easy to use.

In addition to optimizing your guide for the content of the test, we've outlined our recommended steps for breaking down the preparation process into small, attainable goals so you can make sure you stay on track.

We've also analyzed the entire test-taking process, identifying the most common pitfalls and showing how you can overcome them and be ready for any curveball the test throws you.

Standardized testing is one of the biggest obstacles on your road to success, which only increases the importance of doing well in the high-pressure, high-stakes environment of test day. Your results on this test could have a significant impact on your future, and this guide provides the information and practical advice to help you achieve your full potential on test day.

Your success is our success

We would love to hear from you! If you would like to share the story of your exam success or if you have any questions or comments in regard to our products, please contact us at **800-673-8175** or **support@mometrix.com**.

Thanks again for your business and we wish you continued success!

Sincerely,
The Mometrix Test Preparation Team

Written and edited by the Mometrix Test Preparation Team
Printed in the United States of America

TABLE OF CONTENTS

Introduction

Thank you for purchasing this resource! You have made the choice to prepare yourself for a test that could have a huge impact on your future, and this guide is designed to help you be fully ready for test day. Obviously, it's important to have a solid understanding of the test material, but you also need to be prepared for the unique environment and stressors of the test, so that you can perform to the best of your abilities.

For this purpose, the first section that appears in this guide is the **Success Strategies**. We've devoted countless hours to meticulously researching what works and what doesn't, and we've boiled down our findings to the five most impactful steps you can take to improve your performance on the test. We start at the beginning with study planning and move through the preparation process, all the way to the testing strategies that will help you get the most out of what you know when you're finally sitting in front of the test.

We recommend that you start preparing for your test as far in advance as possible. However, if you've bought this guide as a last-minute study resource and only have a few days before your test, we recommend that you skip over the first two Success Strategies since they address a long-term study plan.

If you struggle with **test anxiety**, we strongly encourage you to check out our recommendations for how you can overcome it. Test anxiety is a formidable foe, but it can be beaten, and we want to make sure you have the tools you need to defeat it.

Strategy #1 – Plan Big, Study Small

There's a lot riding on your performance. If you want to ace this test, you're going to need to keep your skills sharp and the material fresh in your mind. You need a plan that lets you review everything you need to know while still fitting in your schedule. We'll break this strategy down into three categories.

Information Organization

Start with the information you already have: the official test outline. From this, you can make a complete list of all the concepts you need to cover before the test. Organize these concepts into groups that can be studied together, and create a list of any related vocabulary you need to learn so you can brush up on any difficult terms. You'll want to keep this vocabulary list handy once you actually start studying since you may need to add to it along the way.

Time Management

Once you have your set of study concepts, decide how to spread them out over the time you have left before the test. Break your study plan into small, clear goals so you have a manageable task for each day and know exactly what you're doing. Then just focus on one small step at a time. When you manage your time this way, you don't need to spend hours at a time studying. Studying a small block of content for a short period each day helps you retain information better and avoid stressing over how much you have left to do. You can relax knowing that you have a plan to cover everything in time. In order for this strategy to be effective though, you have to start studying early and stick to your schedule. Avoid the exhaustion and futility that comes from last-minute cramming!

Study Environment

The environment you study in has a big impact on your learning. Studying in a coffee shop, while probably more enjoyable, is not likely to be as fruitful as studying in a quiet room. It's important to keep distractions to a minimum. You're only planning to study for a short block of time, so make the most of it. Don't pause to check your phone or get up to find a snack. It's also important to **avoid multitasking**. Research has consistently shown that multitasking will make your studying dramatically less effective. Your study area should also be comfortable and well-lit so you don't have the distraction of straining your eyes or sitting on an uncomfortable chair.

The time of day you study is also important. You want to be rested and alert. Don't wait until just before bedtime. Study when you'll be most likely to comprehend and remember. Even better, if you know what time of day your test will be, set that time aside for study. That way your brain will be used to working on that subject at that specific time and you'll have a better chance of recalling information.

Finally, it can be helpful to team up with others who are studying for the same test. Your actual studying should be done in as isolated an environment as possible, but the work of organizing the information and setting up the study plan can be divided up. In between study sessions, you can discuss with your teammates the concepts that you're all studying and quiz each other on the details. Just be sure that your teammates are as serious about the test as you are. If you find that your study time is being replaced with social time, you might need to find a new team.

Strategy #2 – Make Your Studying Count

You're devoting a lot of time and effort to preparing for this test, so you want to be absolutely certain it will pay off. This means doing more than just reading the content and hoping you can remember it on test day. It's important to make every minute of study count. There are two main areas you can focus on to make your studying count.

Retention

It doesn't matter how much time you study if you can't remember the material. You need to make sure you are retaining the concepts. To check your retention of the information you're learning, try recalling it at later times with minimal prompting. Try carrying around flashcards and glance at one or two from time to time or ask a friend who's also studying for the test to quiz you.

To enhance your retention, look for ways to put the information into practice so that you can apply it rather than simply recalling it. If you're using the information in practical ways, it will be much easier to remember. Similarly, it helps to solidify a concept in your mind if you're not only reading it to yourself but also explaining it to someone else. Ask a friend to let you teach them about a concept you're a little shaky on (or speak aloud to an imaginary audience if necessary). As you try to summarize, define, give examples, and answer your friend's questions, you'll understand the concepts better and they will stay with you longer. Finally, step back for a big picture view and ask yourself how each piece of information fits with the whole subject. When you link the different concepts together and see them working together as a whole, it's easier to remember the individual components.

Finally, practice showing your work on any multi-step problems, even if you're just studying. Writing out each step you take to solve a problem will help solidify the process in your mind, and you'll be more likely to remember it during the test.

Modality

Modality simply refers to the means or method by which you study. Choosing a study modality that fits your own individual learning style is crucial. No two people learn best in exactly the same way, so it's important to know your strengths and use them to your advantage.

For example, if you learn best by visualization, focus on visualizing a concept in your mind and draw an image or a diagram. Try color-coding your notes, illustrating them, or creating symbols that will trigger your mind to recall a learned concept. If you learn best by hearing or discussing information, find a study partner who learns the same way or read aloud to yourself. Think about how to put the information in your own words. Imagine that you are giving a lecture on the topic and record yourself so you can listen to it later.

For any learning style, flashcards can be helpful. Organize the information so you can take advantage of spare moments to review. Underline key words or phrases. Use different colors for different categories. Mnemonic devices (such as creating a short list in which every item starts with the same letter) can also help with retention. Find what works best for you and use it to store the information in your mind most effectively and easily.

Strategy #3 – Practice the Right Way

Your success on test day depends not only on how many hours you put into preparing, but also on whether you prepared the right way. It's good to check along the way to see if your studying is paying off. One of the most effective ways to do this is by taking practice tests to evaluate your progress. Practice tests are useful because they show exactly where you need to improve. Every time you take a practice test, pay special attention to these three groups of questions:

- The questions you got wrong
- The questions you had to guess on, even if you guessed right
- The questions you found difficult or slow to work through

This will show you exactly what your weak areas are, and where you need to devote more study time. Ask yourself why each of these questions gave you trouble. Was it because you didn't understand the material? Was it because you didn't remember the vocabulary? Do you need more repetitions on this type of question to build speed and confidence? Dig into those questions and figure out how you can strengthen your weak areas as you go back to review the material.

Additionally, many practice tests have a section explaining the answer choices. It can be tempting to read the explanation and think that you now have a good understanding of the concept. However, an explanation likely only covers part of the question's broader context. Even if the explanation makes perfect sense, **go back and investigate** every concept related to the question until you're positive you have a thorough understanding.

As you go along, keep in mind that the practice test is just that: practice. Memorizing these questions and answers will not be very helpful on the actual test because it is unlikely to have any of the same exact questions. If you only know the right answers to the sample questions, you won't be prepared for the real thing. **Study the concepts** until you understand them fully, and then you'll be able to answer any question that shows up on the test.

It's important to wait on the practice tests until you're ready. If you take a test on your first day of study, you may be overwhelmed by the amount of material covered and how much you need to learn. Work up to it gradually.

On test day, you'll need to be prepared for answering questions, managing your time, and using the test-taking strategies you've learned. It's a lot to balance, like a mental marathon that will have a big impact on your future. Like training for a marathon, you'll need to start slowly and work your way up. When test day arrives, you'll be ready.

Start with the strategies you've read in the first two Success Strategies—plan your course and study in the way that works best for you. If you have time, consider using multiple study resources to get different approaches to the same concepts. It can be helpful to see difficult concepts from more than one angle. Then find a good source for practice tests. Many times, the test website will suggest potential study resources or provide sample tests.

Practice Test Strategy

If you're able to find at least three practice tests, we recommend this strategy:

Untimed and Open-Book Practice

Take the first test with no time constraints and with your notes and study guide handy. Take your time and focus on applying the strategies you've learned.

Timed and Open-Book Practice

Take the second practice test open-book as well, but set a timer and practice pacing yourself to finish in time.

Timed and Closed-Book Practice

Take any other practice tests as if it were test day. Set a timer and put away your study materials. Sit at a table or desk in a quiet room, imagine yourself at the testing center, and answer questions as quickly and accurately as possible.

Keep repeating timed and closed-book tests on a regular basis until you run out of practice tests or it's time for the actual test. Your mind will be ready for the schedule and stress of test day, and you'll be able to focus on recalling the material you've learned.

Strategy #4 – Pace Yourself

Once you're fully prepared for the material on the test, your biggest challenge on test day will be managing your time. Just knowing that the clock is ticking can make you panic even if you have plenty of time left. Work on pacing yourself so you can build confidence against the time constraints of the exam. Pacing is a difficult skill to master, especially in a high-pressure environment, so **practice is vital**.

Set time expectations for your pace based on how much time is available. For example, if a section has 60 questions and the time limit is 30 minutes, you know you have to average 30 seconds or less per question in order to answer them all. Although 30 seconds is the hard limit, set 25 seconds per question as your goal, so you reserve extra time to spend on harder questions. When you budget extra time for the harder questions, you no longer have any reason to stress when those questions take longer to answer.

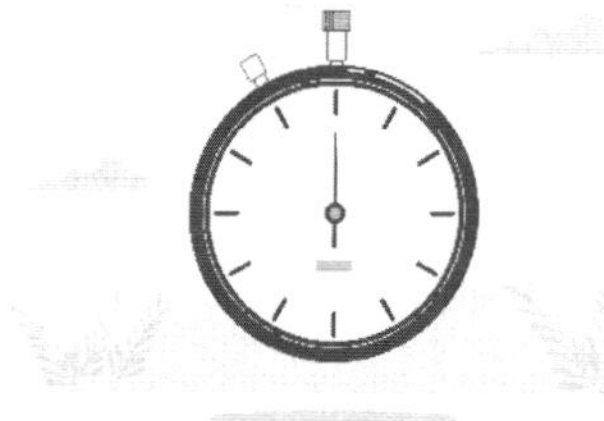

Don't let this time expectation distract you from working through the test at a calm, steady pace, but keep it in mind so you don't spend too much time on any one question. Recognize that taking extra time on one question you don't understand may keep you from answering two that you do understand later in the test. If your time limit for a question is up and you're still not sure of the answer, mark it and move on, and come back to it later if the time and the test format allow. If the testing format doesn't allow you to return to earlier questions, just make an educated guess; then put it out of your mind and move on.

On the easier questions, be careful not to rush. It may seem wise to hurry through them so you have more time for the challenging ones, but it's not worth missing one if you know the concept and just didn't take the time to read the question fully. Work efficiently but make sure you understand the question and have looked at all of the answer choices, since more than one may seem right at first.

Even if you're paying attention to the time, you may find yourself a little behind at some point. You should speed up to get back on track, but do so wisely. Don't panic; just take a few seconds less on each question until you're caught up. Don't guess without thinking, but do look through the answer choices and eliminate any you know are wrong. If you can get down to two choices, it is often worthwhile to guess from those. Once you've chosen an answer, move on and don't dwell on any that you skipped or had to hurry through. If a question was taking too long, chances are it was one of the harder ones, so you weren't as likely to get it right anyway.

On the other hand, if you find yourself getting ahead of schedule, it may be beneficial to slow down a little. The more quickly you work, the more likely you are to make a careless mistake that will affect your score. You've budgeted time for each question, so don't be afraid to spend that time. Practice an efficient but careful pace to get the most out of the time you have.

Test-Taking Strategies

This section contains a list of test-taking strategies that you may find helpful as you work through the test. By taking what you know and applying logical thought, you can maximize your chances of answering any question correctly!

It is very important to realize that every question is different and every person is different: no single strategy will work on every question, and no single strategy will work for every person. That's why we've included all of them here, so you can try them out and determine which ones work best for different types of questions and which ones work best for you.

Question Strategies

✓ Read Carefully

Read the question and the answer choices carefully. Don't miss the question because you misread the terms. You have plenty of time to read each question thoroughly and make sure you understand what is being asked. Yet a happy medium must be attained, so don't waste too much time. You must read carefully and efficiently.

✓ Contextual Clues

Look for contextual clues. If the question includes a word you are not familiar with, look at the immediate context for some indication of what the word might mean. Contextual clues can often give you all the information you need to decipher the meaning of an unfamiliar word. Even if you can't determine the meaning, you may be able to narrow down the possibilities enough to make a solid guess at the answer to the question.

✓ Prefixes

If you're having trouble with a word in the question or answer choices, try dissecting it. Take advantage of every clue that the word might include. Prefixes can be a huge help. Usually, they allow you to determine a basic meaning. *Pre-* means before, *post-* means after, *pro-* is positive, *de-* is negative. From prefixes, you can get an idea of the general meaning of the word and try to put it into context.

✓ Hedge Words

Watch out for critical hedge words, such as *likely, may, can, often, almost, mostly, usually, generally, rarely*, and *sometimes*. Question writers insert these hedge phrases to cover every possibility. Often an answer choice will be wrong simply because it leaves no room for exception. Be on guard for answer choices that have definitive words such as *exactly* and *always*.

✓ Switchback Words

Stay alert for *switchbacks*. These are the words and phrases frequently used to alert you to shifts in thought. The most common switchback words are *but, although*, and *however*. Others include *nevertheless, on the other hand, even though, while, in spite of, despite*, and *regardless of*. Switchback words are important to catch because they can change the direction of the question or an answer choice.

☑ Face Value

When in doubt, use common sense. Accept the situation in the problem at face value. Don't read too much into it. These problems will not require you to make wild assumptions. If you have to go beyond creativity and warp time or space in order to have an answer choice fit the question, then you should move on and consider the other answer choices. These are normal problems rooted in reality. The applicable relationship or explanation may not be readily apparent, but it is there for you to figure out. Use your common sense to interpret anything that isn't clear.

Answer Choice Strategies

☑ Answer Selection

The most thorough way to pick an answer choice is to identify and eliminate wrong answers until only one is left, then confirm it is the correct answer. Sometimes an answer choice may immediately seem right, but be careful. The test writers will usually put more than one reasonable answer choice on each question, so take a second to read all of them and make sure that the other choices are not equally obvious. As long as you have time left, it is better to read every answer choice than to pick the first one that looks right without checking the others.

☑ Answer Choice Families

An answer choice family consists of two (in rare cases, three) answer choices that are very similar in construction and cannot all be true at the same time. If you see two answer choices that are direct opposites or parallels, one of them is usually the correct answer. For instance, if one answer choice says that quantity *x* increases and another either says that quantity *x* decreases (opposite) or says that quantity *y* increases (parallel), then those answer choices would fall into the same family. An answer choice that doesn't match the construction of the answer choice family is more likely to be incorrect. Most questions will not have answer choice families, but when they do appear, you should be prepared to recognize them.

☑ Eliminate Answers

Eliminate answer choices as soon as you realize they are wrong, but make sure you consider all possibilities. If you are eliminating answer choices and realize that the last one you are left with is also wrong, don't panic. Start over and consider each choice again. There may be something you missed the first time that you will realize on the second pass.

☑ Avoid Fact Traps

Don't be distracted by an answer choice that is factually true but doesn't answer the question. You are looking for the choice that answers the question. Stay focused on what the question is asking for so you don't accidentally pick an answer that is true but incorrect. Always go back to the question and make sure the answer choice you've selected actually answers the question and is not merely a true statement.

☑ Extreme Statements

In general, you should avoid answers that put forth extreme actions as standard practice or proclaim controversial ideas as established fact. An answer choice that states the "process should be used in certain situations, if..." is much more likely to be correct than one that states the "process should be discontinued completely." The first is a calm rational statement and doesn't even make a definitive, uncompromising stance, using a hedge word *if* to provide wiggle room, whereas the second choice is far more extreme.

☑ BENCHMARK

As you read through the answer choices and you come across one that seems to answer the question well, mentally select that answer choice. This is not your final answer, but it's the one that will help you evaluate the other answer choices. The one that you selected is your benchmark or standard for judging each of the other answer choices. Every other answer choice must be compared to your benchmark. That choice is correct until proven otherwise by another answer choice beating it. If you find a better answer, then that one becomes your new benchmark. Once you've decided that no other choice answers the question as well as your benchmark, you have your final answer.

☑ PREDICT THE ANSWER

Before you even start looking at the answer choices, it is often best to try to predict the answer. When you come up with the answer on your own, it is easier to avoid distractions and traps because you will know exactly what to look for. The right answer choice is unlikely to be word-for-word what you came up with, but it should be a close match. Even if you are confident that you have the right answer, you should still take the time to read each option before moving on.

General Strategies

☑ TOUGH QUESTIONS

If you are stumped on a problem or it appears too hard or too difficult, don't waste time. Move on! Remember though, if you can quickly check for obviously incorrect answer choices, your chances of guessing correctly are greatly improved. Before you completely give up, at least try to knock out a couple of possible answers. Eliminate what you can and then guess at the remaining answer choices before moving on.

☑ CHECK YOUR WORK

Since you will probably not know every term listed and the answer to every question, it is important that you get credit for the ones that you do know. Don't miss any questions through careless mistakes. If at all possible, try to take a second to look back over your answer selection and make sure you've selected the correct answer choice and haven't made a costly careless mistake (such as marking an answer choice that you didn't mean to mark). This quick double check should more than pay for itself in caught mistakes for the time it costs.

☑ PACE YOURSELF

It's easy to be overwhelmed when you're looking at a page full of questions; your mind is confused and full of random thoughts, and the clock is ticking down faster than you would like. Calm down and maintain the pace that you have set for yourself. Especially as you get down to the last few minutes of the test, don't let the small numbers on the clock make you panic. As long as you are on track by monitoring your pace, you are guaranteed to have time for each question.

☑ DON'T RUSH

It is very easy to make errors when you are in a hurry. Maintaining a fast pace in answering questions is pointless if it makes you miss questions that you would have gotten right otherwise. Test writers like to include distracting information and wrong answers that seem right. Taking a little extra time to avoid careless mistakes can make all the difference in your test score. Find a pace that allows you to be confident in the answers that you select.

✓ Keep Moving

Panicking will not help you pass the test, so do your best to stay calm and keep moving. Taking deep breaths and going through the answer elimination steps you practiced can help to break through a stress barrier and keep your pace.

Final Notes

The combination of a solid foundation of content knowledge and the confidence that comes from practicing your plan for applying that knowledge is the key to maximizing your performance on test day. As your foundation of content knowledge is built up and strengthened, you'll find that the strategies included in this chapter become more and more effective in helping you quickly sift through the distractions and traps of the test to isolate the correct answer.

Now that you're preparing to move forward into the test content chapters of this book, be sure to keep your goal in mind. As you read, think about how you will be able to apply this information on the test. If you've already seen sample questions for the test and you have an idea of the question format and style, try to come up with questions of your own that you can answer based on what you're reading. This will give you valuable practice applying your knowledge in the same ways you can expect to on test day.

Good luck and good studying!

United States History

American History Pre-Columbian to 1789

Prior to European colonization, the land that would become the United States was populated by millions of Native Americans belonging to hundreds of distinct tribes. Native American societies were diverse and sophisticated, with political structures, religious beliefs, domesticated animals, agricultural practices, and trade networks. Native Americans adapted their societies and cultures to the environments in which they settled, which led to distinct cultures, beliefs, practices, and languages all across the continent.

Well-Known Native Americans

The following are five well-known Native Americans and their roles in early US history:

1. **Squanto**, an Algonquian, helped early English settlers survive the hard winter by teaching them the native methods of planting corn, squash, and pumpkins.
2. **Pocahontas**, also Algonquian, became famous as a liaison with John Smith's Jamestown colony in 1607.
3. **Sacagawea**, a Shoshone, served a vital role in the Lewis and Clark expedition when the two explorers hired her as their guide in 1805.
4. **Crazy Horse** and **Sitting Bull** led Sioux and Cheyenne troops in the Battle of the Little Bighorn in 1876, soundly defeating George Armstrong Custer.
5. **Chief Joseph**, a leader of the Nez Perce who supported peaceful interaction with white settlers, attempted to relocate his tribe to Canada rather than move them to a reservation.

Major Regional Native American Groups

The major regional Native American groups and the major traits of each are as follows:

- The **Algonquians** in the eastern part of the United States lived in wigwams. The northern tribes subsisted on hunting and gathering, while those who were farther south grew crops such as corn.
- The **Iroquois**, also an east coast tribe, spoke a different language from the Algonquians and lived in rectangular longhouses.
- The **Plains tribes** lived between the Mississippi River and the Rocky Mountains. These nomadic tribes lived in teepees and followed the buffalo herds. Plains tribes included the Sioux, Cheyenne, Comanche, and Blackfoot.
- **Pueblo tribes** included the Zuni, Hopi, and Acoma. They lived in the Southwest deserts in homes made of stone or adobe. They domesticated animals and cultivated corn and beans.
- On the Pacific coast, tribes such as the **Tlingit**, **Chinook**, and **Salish** lived on fish,deer, native berries, and roots. Their rectangular homes housed large family groups, and they used totem poles.
- In the far north, the **Aleuts** and **Inuit** lived in skin tents or igloos. Talented fishermen, they built kayaks and umiaks and also hunted caribou, seals, whales, and walrus.

Review Video: Major Regional Native American Groups
Visit mometrix.com/academy and enter code: 550136

Age of Exploration

The Age of Exploration is also called the **Age of Discovery**. It is generally considered to have begun in the early 15th century and continued into the 17th century. Major developments of the **Age of Exploration** included technological advances in navigation, mapmaking, and shipbuilding. These advances led to expanded European exploration of the rest of the world. Explorers set out from several European countries, including Portugal, Spain, France, and England, seeking new routes to Asia. These efforts led to the discovery of new lands, as well as colonization in India, Asia, Africa, and North America.

Review Video: Age of Exploration
Visit mometrix.com/academy and enter code: 612972

Impact of Technological Advances in Navigation and Seafaring Exploration

For long ocean journeys, it was important for sailors to be able to find their way home even when their vessels sailed far out to sea. A variety of navigational tools enabled them to launch ambitious journeys over long distances. The **compass** and **astrolabe** were particularly important advancements. Chinese navigators used the magnetic compass in approximately 200 BC, and knowledge of the astrolabe came to Europe from Arab navigators and traders who had refined designs developed by the ancient Greeks. The Portuguese developed a ship called a **caravel** in the 1400s that incorporated navigational advancements with the ability to make long sea journeys. Equipped with this advanced vessel, the Portuguese achieved a major goal of the Age of Exploration by discovering a **sea route** from Europe to Asia in 1498.

Significance of Christopher Columbus's Voyage

In 1492, Columbus, a Genoan explorer, obtained financial backing from King Ferdinand and Queen Isabella of Spain to seek a sea route to Asia. He sought a trade route with the Asian Indies to the west. With three ships, the *Niña*, the *Pinta*, and the *Santa Maria*, he eventually landed in the **West Indies**. While Columbus failed in his effort to discover a western route to Asia, he is credited with the discovery of the **Americas**.

Review Video: Christopher Columbus
Visit mometrix.com/academy and enter code: 496598

French, Spanish, Dutch, and British Goals in Colonization of the Americas

France, Spain, the Netherlands, and England each had specific goals in the colonization of the Americas:

- Initial **French colonies** were focused on expanding the fur trade. Later, French colonization led to the growth of plantations in Louisiana, which brought numerous African slaves to the New World.
- **Spanish colonists** came to look for wealth and to convert the natives to Christianity. For some, the desire for gold led to mining in the New World, while others established large ranches.

- The **Dutch** were also involved in the fur trade and imported slaves as the need for laborers increased.
- **British colonists** arrived with various goals. Some were simply looking for additional income, while others were fleeing Britain to escape religious persecution.

Review Video: European Colonization of the Americas
Visit mometrix.com/academy and enter code: 438412

Interactions Between the Colonies and Native Americans

While there were examples of peaceful relations between Native Americans and European colonists, these two groups were often in conflict. The colonists constantly attempted to expand their territories and take Native American land. Native Americans often tried to stop the expansion of European colonies via war and diplomacy, both of which usually resulted in failure due to European advantages in technology and shifting alliances. Both the colonists and the Native Americans committed atrocities against the other in these conflicts. Many Native Americans captured in war were made slaves; however, the most fatal attack suffered by the Native Americans came in the form of disease. Foreign diseases like small pox ravaged through the Native American population. Some researchers estimate that up to 90% of the Native American population died as a result of foreign diseases brought to America by colonists.

New England Colonies

The New England colonies were New Hampshire, Connecticut, Rhode Island and Massachusetts. These colonies were founded largely to escape **religious persecution** in England. The beliefs of the **Puritans**, who migrated to America in the 1600s, significantly influenced the development of these colonies. Situated in the northeast coastal areas of America, the New England colonies featured numerous harbors as well as dense forests. The soil, however, was rocky and had a very short growing season, so was not well suited for agriculture. The economy of New England during the colonial period centered around fishing, shipbuilding and trade along with some small farms and lumber mills. Although some groups congregated in small farms, life centered mainly in towns and cities where **merchants** largely controlled the trade economy. Coastal cities such as Boston grew and thrived.

Review Video: The Massachusetts Bay Colony
Visit mometrix.com/academy and enter code: 407058

Middle or Middle Atlantic Colonies

The Middle or Middle Atlantic Colonies were New York, New Jersey, Pennsylvania, and Delaware. Unlike the New England colonies, where most colonists were from England and Scotland, the Middle Colonies founders were from various countries, including the Netherlands and Sweden. Various factors led these colonists to America. More fertile than New England, the Middle Colonies became major producers of **crops**, including rye, oats, potatoes, wheat, and barley. Some particularly wealthy inhabitants owned large farms and/or businesses. Farmers, in general, were able to produce enough to have a surplus to sell. Tenant farmers also rented land from larger landowners.

Southern Colonies

The Southern Colonies were Maryland, Virginia, North Carolina, South Carolina, and Georgia. Of the Southern Colonies, Virginia was the first permanent English colony and Georgia the last. The warm climate and rich soil of the south encouraged **agriculture**, and the growing season was long. As a result, economy in the south was based largely on labor-intensive **plantations**. Crops included tobacco, rice, and indigo, all of which became valuable cash crops. Most land in the south was controlled by wealthy plantation owners and farmers. Labor on the farms came in the form of indentured servants and African slaves. The first of these **African slaves** arrived in Virginia in 1619.

> **Review Video: The Southern Colonies**
> Visit mometrix.com/academy and enter code: 703830
>
> **Review Video: The English Colony of Virginia**
> Visit mometrix.com/academy and enter code: 537399

Significance of the French and Indian Wars

The **British defeat of the Spanish Armada** in 1588 led to the decline of Spanish power in Europe. This, in turn, led the British and French into battle several times between 1689 and 1748. These wars were:

- King William's War, or the Nine Years War, 1689-1697. This war was fought largely in Flanders.
- The War of Spanish Succession, or Queen Anne's War, 1702-1713
- War of Austrian Succession, or King George's War, 1740-1748

The fourth and final war, the **French and Indian War** (1754-1763), was fought largely in the North American territory and resulted in the end of France's reign as a colonial power in North America. Although the French held many advantages, including more cooperative colonists and numerous Native American allies, the strong leadership of **William Pitt** eventually led the British to victory. Costs incurred during the wars eventually led to discontent in the colonies and helped spark the **American Revolution**.

> **Review Video: French and Indian Wars**
> Visit mometrix.com/academy and enter code: 502183

Navigation Acts

The Navigation Acts, enacted in 1651, were an attempt by Britain to dominate international trade. Aimed largely at the Dutch, the acts banned foreign ships from transporting goods to the British colonies and from transporting goods to Britain from elsewhere in Europe. While the restrictions on trade angered some colonists, these acts were helpful to other American colonists who, as members of the British Empire, were legally able to provide ships for Britain's growing trade interests and use the ships for their own trading ventures. By the time the French and Indian War had ended, one-third of British merchant ships were built in the American colonies. Many colonists amassed fortunes in the shipbuilding trade.

Acts of British Parliament that Occurred After the French and Indian Wars

After the French and Indian Wars, the British Parliament passed four major acts:

1. The **Sugar Act**, 1764—this act not only required taxes to be collected on molasses brought into the colonies but gave British officials the right to search the homes of anyone suspected of violating it.

2. The **Stamp Act**, 1765—this act taxed printed materials such as newspapers and legal documents. Protests led the Stamp Act to be repealed in 1766, but the repeal also included the Declaratory Act, which stated that Parliament had the right to govern the colonies.
3. The **Quartering Act**, 1765—this act required colonists to provide accommodations and supplies for British troops. In addition, colonists were prohibited from settling west of the Appalachians until given permission by Britain.
4. The **Townshend Acts**, 1767—these acts taxed paper, paint, lead, and tea that came into the colonies. Colonists led boycotts in protest, and in Massachusetts leaders like Samuel and John Adams began to organize resistance against British rule.

Britain's Taxation of the American Colonies After the French and Indian War

The French and Indian War created circumstances for which the British desperately needed more revenue. These needs included:

- Paying off the war debt
- Defending the expanding empire
- Governing Britain's 33 far-flung colonies, including the American colonies

To meet these needs, the British passed additional laws, increasing revenues from the colonies. Because they had spent so much money to defend the American colonies, the British felt it was appropriate to collect considerably higher **taxes** from them. The colonists felt this was unfair, and many were led to protest the increasing taxes. Eventually, protest led to violence.

Triangular Trade

Triangular trade began in the colonies with ships setting off for **Africa**, carrying rum. In Africa, the rum was traded for gold or slaves. Ships then went from Africa to the **West Indies**, trading slaves for sugar, molasses, or money. To complete the triangle, the ships returned to the **colonies** with sugar or molasses to make more rum, as well as stores of gold and silver. This trade triangle violated the Molasses Act of 1733, which required the colonists to pay high duties to Britain on molasses acquired from French, Dutch, and Spanish colonies. The colonists ignored these duties, and the British government adopted a policy of salutary neglect by not enforcing them.

Review Video: The Triangular Trade
Visit mometrix.com/academy and enter code: 415470

Effects of New Laws on British-Colonial Relations

While earlier revenue-generating acts such as the Navigation Acts brought money to the colonists, the new laws after 1763 required colonists to pay money back to **Britain**. The British felt this was fair since the colonists were British subjects and since they had incurred debt protecting the Colonies. The colonists felt it was not only unfair but illegal.

The development of **local government** in America had given the colonists a different view of the structure and role of government. This made it difficult for the British to understand the colonists' protests against what the British felt was a fair and reasonable solution to the mother country's financial problems.

Factors that Led to Increasing Discontent in the American Colonies

More and more colonists were born on American soil, decreasing any sense of kinship with the far-away British rulers. Their new environment had led to new ideas of government and a strong view of the colonies as a separate entity from Britain. Colonists were allowed to **self-govern** in domestic issues, but **Britain** controlled international issues. In fact, the American colonies were largely left to form their own local government bodies, giving them more freedom than any other colonial territory. This gave the colonists a sense of **independence**, which led them to resent control from Britain. Threats during the French and Indian War led the colonists to call for unification in order to protect themselves.

Colonial and British Government Differences That Caused Tension

As new towns and other legislative districts developed in America, the colonists began to practice **representative government**. Colonial legislative bodies were made up of elected representatives chosen by male property owners in the districts. These individuals represented the interests of the districts from which they had been elected.

By contrast, in Britain, the **Parliament** represented the entire country. Parliament was not elected to represent individual districts. Instead, they represented specific classes. Because of this drastically different approach to government, the British did not understand the colonists' statement that they had no representation in the British Parliament.

Factors That Led to the Boston Massacre

With the passage of the **Stamp Act**, nine colonies met in New York to demand its repeal. Elsewhere, protest arose in New York City, Philadelphia, Boston, and other cities. These protests sometimes escalated into violence, often targeting ruling British officials. The passage of the **Townshend Acts** in 1767 led to additional tension in the colonies. The British sent troops to New York City and Boston. On March 5, 1770, protesters began to taunt the British troops, throwing snowballs. The soldiers responded by firing into the crowd. This clash between protesters and soldiers led to five deaths and eight injuries, and was christened the **Boston Massacre**. Shortly thereafter, Britain repealed the majority of the Townshend Acts.

Tea Act That Led to the Boston Tea Party

The majority of the **Townshend Acts** were repealed after the Boston Massacre in 1770, but Britain kept the tax on tea. In 1773, the **Tea Act** was passed. This allowed the East India Company to sell tea for much lower prices and also allowed them to bypass American distributors, selling directly to shopkeepers instead. Colonial tea merchants saw this as a direct assault on their business. In December of 1773, the **Sons of Liberty** boarded ships in Boston Harbor and dumped 342 chests of tea into the sea in protest of the new laws. This act of protest came to be known as the **Boston Tea Party**.

Coercive Acts Passed after the Boston Tea Party

The Coercive Acts passed by Britain in 1774 were meant to punish Massachusetts for defying British authority. These became collectively known as the **Intolerable Acts** in the colonies and mandated the following:

- Shut down ports in Boston until the city paid back the value of the tea destroyed during the Boston Tea Party
- Required that local government officials in Massachusetts be appointed by the governor rather than being elected by the people
- Allowed trials of British soldiers to be transferred to Britain rather than being held in Massachusetts
- Required locals to provide lodging for British soldiers any time there was a disturbance, even if lodging required them to stay in private homes

These acts led to the assembly of the First Continental Congress in Philadelphia on September 5, 1774. Fifty-five delegates met, representing 12 of the American colonies. They sought compromise with England over England's increasingly harsh efforts to control the colonies.

First Continental Congress

The goal of the First Continental Congress was to achieve a peaceful agreement with Britain. Made up of delegates from 12 of the 13 colonies, the Congress affirmed loyalty to Britain and the power of Parliament to dictate foreign affairs in the colonies. However, they demanded that the **Intolerable Acts** be repealed, and instituted a trade embargo with Britain until this came to pass.

In response, George III of England declared that the American colonies must submit or face military action. The British sought to end assemblies that opposed their policies. These assemblies gathered weapons and began to form militias. On April 19, 1775, the British military was ordered to disperse a meeting of the Massachusetts Assembly. A battle ensued on Lexington Common as the armed colonists resisted. The resulting battles became the **Battle of Lexington and Concord**—the first battles of the **American Revolution**.

Significance of the Second Continental Congress

The Second Continental Congress met in Philadelphia on May 10, 1775, a month after Lexington and Concord. Their discussions centered on the defense of the American colonies and how to conduct the growing war, as well as local government. The delegates also discussed declaring independence from Britain, with many members in favor of this drastic move. They established an army, and on June 15, named **George Washington** as its commander in chief. By 1776, it was obvious that there was no turning back from full-scale war with Britain. The colonial delegates of the Continental Congress signed the **Declaration of Independence** on July 4, 1776.

Review Video: The First and Second Continental Congress
Visit mometrix.com/academy and enter code: 835211

Origins and Basic Ideas of the Declaration of Independence

Penned by Thomas Jefferson and signed on July 4, 1776, the **Declaration of Independence** stated that King George III had violated the rights of the colonists and was establishing a tyrannical reign over them. Many of Jefferson's ideas of natural rights and property rights were shaped by 17th-century philosopher **John Locke**. Jefferson asserted all people's rights to "life, liberty and the pursuit of happiness." Locke's comparable idea asserted "life, liberty, and private property." Both felt that the purpose of government was to protect the rights of the people, and that individual rights were more important than individuals' obligations to the state.

Review Video: Declaration of Independence
Visit mometrix.com/academy and enter code: 256838

Battles of the Revolutionary War

The following are five major battles of the Revolutionary War and their significance:

- The **Battle of Lexington and Concord** (April 1775) is considered the first engagement of the Revolutionary War.
- The **Battle of Bunker Hill** (June 1775) was one of the bloodiest of the entire war. Although American troops withdrew, about half of the British army was lost. The colonists proved they could stand against professional British soldiers. In August, Britain declared that the American colonies were officially in a state of rebellion.

- The first colonial victory occurred in Trenton, New Jersey, when Washington and his troops **crossed the Delaware River** on Christmas Day, 1776, for a December 26 surprise attack on British and Hessian troops.
- The **Battle of Saratoga** effectively ended a plan to separate the New England colonies from their Southern counterparts. The surrender of British general John Burgoyne led to France joining the war as allies of the Americans and is generally considered a turning point of the war.
- On October 19, 1781, General Cornwallis surrendered after a defeat in the **Battle of Yorktown**, ending the Revolutionary War.

Review Video: The American Revolutionary War
Visit mometrix.com/academy and enter code: 935282

Significance of the Treaty of Paris

The Treaty of Paris was signed on September 3, 1783, bringing an official end to the Revolutionary War. In this document, Britain officially recognized the United States of America as an **independent nation**. The treaty established the Mississippi River as the country's western border. The treaty also restored Florida to Spain, while France reclaimed African and Caribbean colonies seized by the British in 1763. On November 25, 1783, the last British troops departed from the newly born United States of America.

Significance of the Articles of Confederation

A precursor to the Constitution, the **Articles of Confederation** represented the first attempt of the newly independent colonies to establish the basics of government. The Continental Congress approved the Articles on November 15, 1777. They went into effect on March 1, 1781, following ratification by the thirteen states. The articles prevented a central government from gaining too much power, instead giving power to a **congressional body** made up of **delegates** from all thirteen states. However, the individual states retained final authority.

Without a strong central **executive**, though, this weak alliance among the new states proved ineffective in settling disputes or enforcing laws. The idea of a weak central government needed to be revised. Recognition of these weaknesses eventually led to the drafting of a new document, the **Constitution**.

Review Video: Articles of Confederation
Visit mometrix.com/academy and enter code: 927401

Initial Proposition and Draft of the Constitution

Delegates from twelve of the thirteen states (Rhode Island was not represented) met in Philadelphia in May of 1787, initially intending to revise the Articles of Confederation. However, it quickly became apparent that a simple revision would not provide the workable governmental structure the newly formed country needed. After vowing to keep all the proceedings secret until the final document was completed, the delegates set out to draft what would eventually become the **Constitution of the United States of America**. By keeping the negotiations secret, the delegates were able to present a completed document to the country for ratification, rather than having every small detail hammered out by the general public.

General Structure of Government Proposed by the Delegates

The delegates agreed that the new nation required a **strong central government** but that its overall power should be **limited**. The various branches of the government should have **balanced**

power, so that no one group could control the others. Final power belonged to the **citizens** who voted officials into office based on who would provide the best representation.

OBJECTIONS AGAINST THE CONSTITUTION

Once the Constitution was drafted, it was presented for approval by the states. Nine states needed to approve the document for it to become official. However, debate and discussion continued. Major **concerns** included:

- There was no bill of rights to protect individual freedoms.
- States felt too much power was being handed over to the central government.
- Voters wanted more control over their elected representatives.

Discussion about necessary changes to the Constitution was divided into two camps: Federalists and Anti-Federalists. **Federalists** wanted a strong central government. **Anti-Federalists** wanted to prevent a tyrannical government from developing if a central government held too much power

MAJOR PLAYERS IN THE FEDERALIST AND ANTI-FEDERALIST CAMPS

Major Federalist leaders included Alexander Hamilton, John Jay, and James Madison. They wrote a series of letters, called the **Federalist Papers**, aimed at convincing the states to ratify the Constitution. These were published in New York papers. Anti-Federalists included Thomas Jefferson and Patrick Henry. They argued against the Constitution as it was originally drafted in a series of **Anti-Federalist Papers**.

The final compromise produced a strong central government controlled by checks and balances. A **Bill of Rights** was also added, becoming the first ten amendments to the Constitution. These amendments protected rights such as freedom of speech, freedom of religion, and other basic rights. Aside from various amendments added throughout the years, the United States Constitution has remained unchanged.

INDIVIDUALS WHO FORMED THE FIRST ADMINISTRATION OF THE NEW GOVERNMENT

The individuals who formed the first administration of the new government were:

- **George Washington**—elected as the first President of the United States in 1789
- **John Adams**—finished second in the election and became the first Vice President
- **Thomas Jefferson**—appointed by Washington as Secretary of State
- **Alexander Hamilton**—appointed Secretary of the Treasury

THE VIRGINIA PLAN, THE NEW JERSEY PLAN, AND THE GREAT COMPROMISE

Disagreement immediately occurred between delegates from large states and those from smaller states. James Madison and Edmund Randolph (the governor of Virginia) felt that representation in Congress should be based on state population. This was the **Virginia Plan**. The **New Jersey Plan**, presented by William Paterson from New Jersey, proposed that each state should have equal representation. Finally, Roger Sherman from Connecticut formulated the **Connecticut Compromise**, also called the Great Compromise. The result was the familiar structure we have today. Each state has the equal representation of two Senators in the Senate, with the number of representatives in the House of Representatives based on population. This is called a **bicameral congress**. Both houses may draft bills, but financial matters must originate in the House of Representatives.

The Three-fifths Compromise and Number of Representatives for Each State

During debate on the US Constitution, a disagreement arose between the Northern and Southern states involving how **slaves** should be counted when determining a state's quota of representatives. In the South, large numbers of slaves were commonly used to run plantations. Delegates wanted slaves to be counted to determine the number of representatives but not counted to determine the amount of taxes the states would pay. The Northern states wanted exactly the opposite arrangement. The final decision was to count three-fifths of the slave population both for tax purposes and to determine representation. This was called the **Three-fifths Compromise**.

Provisions of the Commerce Compromise

The Commerce Compromise also resulted from a North/South disagreement. In the North, the economy was centered on **industry and trade**. The Southern economy was largely **agricultural**. The Northern states wanted to give the new government the ability to regulate exports as well as trade between the states. The South opposed this plan. Another compromise was in order. In the end, Congress received regulatory power over all trade, including the ability to collect **tariffs** on exported goods. In the South, this raised another red flag regarding the slave trade, as they were concerned about the effect on their economy if tariffs were levied on slaves. The final agreement allowed importing slaves to continue for twenty years without government intervention. Import taxes on slaves were limited, and after the year 1808, Congress could decide whether to allow continued imports of slaves.

American History 1790 to 1898

Alien and Sedition Acts

When **John Adams** became president, a war was raging between Britain and France. While Adams and the Federalists backed the British, Thomas Jefferson and the Democratic-Republican Party supported the French. The United States nearly went to war with France during this time period, while France worked to spread its international standing and influence under the leadership of **Napoleon Bonaparte**. The **Alien and Sedition Acts** grew out of this conflict and made it illegal to speak in a hostile fashion against the existing government. They also allowed the president to deport anyone in the US who was not a citizen and who was suspected of treason or treasonous activity. When Jefferson became the third president in 1800, he repealed these four laws and pardoned anyone who had been convicted under them.

Development of Political Parties in Early US Government

Many in the US were against political parties after seeing the way parties, or factions, functioned in Britain. The factions in Britain were more interested in personal profit than the overall good of the country, and they did not want this to happen in the US.

However, the differences of opinion between Thomas Jefferson and Alexander Hamilton led to the formation of **political parties**. Hamilton favored a stronger central government, while Jefferson felt that more power should remain with the states. Jefferson was in favor of strict Constitutional interpretation, while Hamilton believed in a more flexible approach. As others joined the two camps, Hamilton backers began to call themselves **Federalists**, while those supporting Jefferson became identified as **Democratic-Republicans**.

Development of the Whig, the Democratic, and the Republican Parties

Thomas Jefferson was elected president in 1800 and again in 1804. The **Federalist Party** began to decline, and its major figure, Alexander Hamilton, died in a duel with Aaron Burr in 1804. By 1816, the Federalist Party had virtually disappeared.

New parties sprang up to take its place. After 1824, the **Democratic-Republican Party** suffered a split. The **Whigs** rose, backing John Quincy Adams and industrial growth. The new Democratic Party formed in opposition to the Whigs, and their candidate, Andrew Jackson, was elected as president in 1828.

By the 1850s, issues regarding slavery led to the formation of the **Republican Party**, which was anti-slavery, while the Democratic Party, with a larger interest in the South, favored slavery. This Republican/Democrat division formed the basis of today's **two-party system**.

Significance of Marbury v. Madison

The main duty of the Supreme Court today is **judicial review**. This power was largely established by **Marbury v. Madison**. When John Adams was voted out of office in 1800, he worked during his final days in office to appoint Federalist judges to Supreme Court positions, knowing Jefferson, his replacement, held opposing views. As late as March 3, the day before Jefferson was to take office, Adams made last-minute appointments referred to as "Midnight Judges." One of the late appointments was William Marbury. The next day, March 4, Jefferson ordered his Secretary of State, James Madison, not to deliver Marbury's commission. This decision was backed by Chief Justice Marshall, who determined that the **Judiciary Act of 1789**, which granted the power to deliver commissions, was illegal in that it gave the Judicial Branch powers not granted in the Constitution. This case set precedent for the Supreme Court to nullify laws it found to be **unconstitutional**.

Review Video: Marbury v Madison
Visit mometrix.com/academy and enter code: 573964

Political Motivations Behind France Selling the Louisiana Purchase

With tension still high between France and Britain, Napoleon was in need of money to support his continuing war efforts. To secure necessary funds, he decided to sell the **Louisiana Territory** to the US. President **Thomas Jefferson** wanted to buy New Orleans, feeling US trade was made vulnerable to both Spain and France at that port. Instead, Napoleon sold him the entire territory for the bargain price of $15 million. The Louisiana Territory was larger than all the rest of the United States put together, and it eventually became 15 additional states.

Federalists in Congress were opposed to the purchase. They feared that the Louisiana Purchase would extend slavery, and that further western growth would weaken the power of the northern states.

Lewis and Clark Expedition

The purchase of the **Louisiana Territory** from France in 1803 more than doubled the size of the United States. President Thomas Jefferson wanted to have the area mapped and explored, since much of the territory was wilderness. He chose Meriwether Lewis and William Clark to head an expedition into the Louisiana Territory. After two years, Lewis and Clark returned, having traveled all the way to the Pacific Ocean. They brought maps, detailed journals, and a multitude of information about the wide expanse of land they had traversed. The **Lewis and Clark Expedition** opened up the west in the Louisiana Territory and beyond for further exploration and settlement.

Review Video: Purpose of the Lewis and Clark Expedition
Visit mometrix.com/academy and enter code: 570657

Causes and Result of the War of 1812

The War of 1812 grew out of the continuing tension between France and Great Britain. Napoleon continued striving to conquer Britain, while the US continued trade with both countries but favored France and the French colonies. Because of what Britain saw as an alliance between America and France, they determined to bring an end to trade between the two nations.

With the British preventing US trade with the French and the French preventing trade with the British, James Madison's presidency introduced acts to **regulate international trade**. If either Britain or France removed their restrictions, America would not trade with the other country. Napoleon acted first, and Madison prohibited trade with England. England saw this as the US formally siding with the French, and war ensued in 1812.

The **War of 1812** has been called the **Second American Revolution**. It established the superiority of the US naval forces and reestablished US independence from Britain and Europe.

The British had two major objections to America's continued trade with France. First, they saw the US as helping France's war effort by providing supplies and goods. Second, the United States had grown into a competitor, taking trade and money away from British ships and tradesmen. In its attempts to end American trade with France, the British put into effect the **Orders in Council**, which made any and all French-owned ports off-limits to American ships. They also began to seize American ships and conscript their crews.

Review Video: Overview of the War of 1812
Visit mometrix.com/academy and enter code: 507716

Review Video: Opinions About the War of 1812
Visit mometrix.com/academy and enter code: 274558

Major Military Events of the War of 1812

Two major naval battles, at **Lake Erie** and **Lake Champlain**, kept the British from invading the US via Canada. American attempts to conquer Canadian lands were not successful.

In another memorable British attack, the British invaded Washington, DC and burned the White House on August 24, 1814. Legend has it that **Dolley Madison**, the First Lady, salvaged the portrait of George Washington from the fire. On Christmas Eve, 1814, the **Treaty of Ghent** officially ended the war. However, Andrew Jackson, unaware that the war was over, managed another victory at New Orleans on January 8, 1815. This victory improved American morale and led to a new wave of national pride and support known as the "**Era of Good Feelings**."

Influence of the American System on American Economics

Spurred by the trade conflicts of the War of 1812 and supported by Henry Clay among others, the **American System** set up tariffs to help protect American interests from competition with overseas products. Reducing competition led to growth in employment and an overall increase in American industry. The higher tariffs also provided funds for the government to pay for various improvements. Congress passed high tariffs in 1816 and also chartered a federal bank. The **Second Bank of the United States** was given the job of regulating America's money supply.

McCulloch v. Maryland

Judicial review was further exercised by the Supreme Court in **McCulloch v. Maryland**. When Congress chartered a national bank, the **Second Bank of the United States**, Maryland voted to tax any bank business dealing with banks chartered outside the state, including the federally chartered bank. Andrew McCulloch, an employee of the Second Bank of the US in Baltimore, refused to pay this tax. The resulting lawsuit from the State of Maryland went to the Supreme Court for judgment.

John Marshall, Chief Justice of the Supreme Court, stated that Congress was within its rights to charter a national bank. In addition, the State of Maryland did not have the power to levy a tax on the federal bank or on the federal government in general. In cases where state and federal government collided, precedent was set for the **federal government** to prevail.

Effects of the Missouri Compromise on the Tensions Between the North and South

By 1819, the United States had developed a tenuous balance between slave and free states, with exactly 22 senators in Congress from each faction. However, Missouri was ready to join the union. As a slave state, it would tip the balance in Congress. To prevent this imbalance, the **Missouri Compromise** brought the northern part of Massachusetts into the union as Maine, establishing it as a free state to balance the admission of Missouri as a slave state. In addition, the remaining portion of the Louisiana Purchase was to remain free north of **latitude 36°30'**. Since cotton did not grow well this far north, this limitation was acceptable to congressmen representing the slave states.

However, the proposed Missouri constitution presented a problem, as it outlawed immigration of free blacks into the state. Another compromise was in order, this time proposed by **Henry Clay**. According to this new compromise, Missouri would never pass a law that prevented anyone from entering the state. Through this and other work, Clay earned his title of the "**Great Compromiser**."

Review Video: The Missouri Compromise
Visit mometrix.com/academy and enter code: 848091

Monroe Doctrine

On December 2, 1823, President Monroe delivered a message to Congress in which he introduced the **Monroe Doctrine**. In this address, he stated that any attempts by European powers to establish new colonies on the North American continent would be considered interference in American politics. The US would stay out of European matters, and expected Europe to offer America the same courtesy. This approach to foreign policy stated in no uncertain terms that America would not tolerate any new European colonies in the New World, and that events occurring in Europe would no longer influence the policies and doctrines of the US.

Review Video: What was the Monroe Doctrine?
Visit mometrix.com/academy and enter code: 953021

Effect of the Treaty of Paris on Native Americans

After the Revolutionary War, the **Treaty of Paris**, which outlined the terms of surrender of the British to the Americans, granted large parcels of land to the US that were occupied by Native Americans. The new government attempted to claim the land, treating the natives as a conquered people. This approach proved unenforceable.

Next, the government tried purchasing the land from the Native Americans via a series of **treaties** as the country expanded westward. In practice, however, these treaties were not honored, and Native Americans were simply dislocated and forced to move farther and farther west, often with military action, as American expansion continued.

Indian Removal Act of 1830 and the Treaty of New Echota

The Indian Removal Act of 1830 gave the new American government power to form treaties with Native Americans. In theory, America would claim land east of the Mississippi in exchange for land west of the Mississippi, to which the natives would relocate voluntarily. In practice, many tribal leaders were forced into signing the treaties, and relocation at times occurred by force.

The **Treaty of New Echota** in 1835 was supposedly a treaty between the US government and Cherokee tribes in Georgia. However, the treaty was not signed by tribal leaders but rather by a small portion of the represented people. The leaders protested and refused to leave, but President Martin Van Buren enforced the treaty by sending soldiers. During their forced relocation, more than 4,000 Cherokees died on what became known as the **Trail of Tears**.

Review Video: Indian Removal Act
Visit mometrix.com/academy and enter code: 666738

Jacksonian Democracy vs. Preceding Political Climate

Jacksonian Democracy is largely seen as a shift from politics favoring the wealthy to politics favoring the common man. The right to vote was given to all free white males, not just property owners, as had been the case previously. Jackson's approach favored the patronage system, laissez-faire economics, and relocation of the Native American tribes from the Southeast portion of the country. Jackson opposed the formation of a federal bank and allowed the Second Bank of the United States to collapse by vetoing a bill to renew the charter. Jackson also faced the challenge of the **Nullification Crisis** when South Carolina claimed that it could ignore or nullify any federal law it considered unconstitutional. Jackson sent troops to the state to enforce the protested tariff laws, and a compromise engineered by Henry Clay in 1833 settled the matter for the time being.

Second Great Awakening

Led by Protestant evangelical leaders, the **Second Great Awakening** occurred between 1800 and 1830. Several missionary groups grew out of the movement, including the **American Home Missionary Society**, which formed in 1826. The ideas behind the Second Great Awakening focused on personal responsibility, both as an individual and in response to injustice and suffering. The **American Bible Society** and the **American Tract Society** provided literature, while various traveling preachers spread the word. New denominations arose, including the Latter-day Saints and Seventh-day Adventists.

Another movement associated with the Second Great Awakening was the **temperance movement**, focused on ending the production and use of alcohol. One major organization behind the temperance movement was the **Society for the Promotion of Temperance**, formed in 1826 in Boston.

Attitudes Toward Education in the Early 19th Century

Horace Mann, among others, felt that schools could help children become better citizens, keep them away from crime, prevent poverty, and help American society become more unified. His *Common School Journal* brought his ideas of the importance of education into the public consciousness and proposed his suggestions for an improved American education system.

Increased literacy led to increased awareness of current events, Western expansion, and other major developments of the time period. Public interest and participation in the arts and literature also increased. By the end of the 19th century, all children had access to a **free public elementary education**.

Development of Economic Trends as the US Continued to Grow

In the Northeast, the economy mostly depended on **manufacturing, industry, and industrial development**. This led to a dichotomy between rich business owners and industrial leaders and the much poorer workers who supported their businesses. The South continued to depend on **agriculture**, especially on large-scale farms or plantations worked mostly by slaves and indentured servants. In the West, where new settlements had begun to develop, the land was largely wild. Growing communities were essentially **agricultural**, raising crops and livestock. The differences between regions led each to support different interests both politically and economically.

Industrial Activity Before and After 1800

During the 18th century, goods were often manufactured in houses or small shops. With increased technology allowing for the use of machines, **factories** began to develop. In factories, a large volume of salable goods could be produced in a much shorter amount of time. Many Americans, including increasing numbers of **immigrants**, found jobs in these factories, which were in constant need of labor. Another major invention was the **cotton gin**, which significantly decreased the processing time of cotton and was a major factor in the rapid expansion of cotton production in the South.

Development of Labor Movements in the 1800s

In 1751, a group of bakers held a protest in which they stopped baking bread. This was technically the first American **labor strike**. In the 1830s and 1840s, labor movements began in earnest. Boston's masons, carpenters, and stoneworkers protested the length of the workday, fighting to reduce it to ten hours. In 1844, a group of women in the textile industry also fought to reduce their workday to ten hours, forming the **Lowell Female Labor Reform Association**. Many other protests occurred and organizations developed through this time period with the same goal in mind.

Major Ideas Driving American Foreign Policy

The three major ideas driving American foreign policy during its early years were:

- **Isolationism**—the early US government did not intend to establish colonies, though they did plan to grow larger within the bounds of North America.
- **No entangling alliances**—both George Washington and Thomas Jefferson were opposed to forming any permanent alliances with other countries or becoming involved in other countries' internal issues.
- **Nationalism**—a positive patriotic feeling about the United States blossomed quickly among its citizens, particularly after the War of 1812, when the US once again defeated Britain. The Industrial Revolution also sparked increased nationalism by allowing even the most far-flung areas of the US to communicate with each other via telegraph and the expanding railroad.

Effects of Manifest Destiny on American Politics

In the 1800s, many believed America was destined by God to expand west, bringing as much of the North American continent as possible under the umbrella of the US government. With the Northwest Ordinance and the Louisiana Purchase, over half of the continent became American.

However, the rapid and relentless expansion brought conflict with the Native Americans, Great Britain, Mexico, and Spain. One result of "**Manifest Destiny**" was the **Mexican-American War** from 1846 to 1848. By the end of the war, Texas, California, and a large portion of what is now the American Southwest joined the growing nation. Conflict also arose over the **Oregon Territory**, shared by the US and Britain. In 1846, President James Polk resolved this problem by compromising with Britain, establishing a US boundary south of the 49th parallel.

Review Video: Manifest Destiny
Visit mometrix.com/academy and enter code: 957409

Mexican-American War

Spain had held colonial interests in America since the 1540s—earlier even than Great Britain. In 1810, **Mexico** revolted against Spain, becoming a free nation in 1821. **Texas** followed suit, declaring its independence after an 1836 revolution. In 1844, the Democrats pressed President Tyler to annex Texas. Unlike his predecessor, Andrew Jackson, Tyler agreed to admit Texas into the Union, and in 1845, Texas became a state.

During Mexico's war for independence, the nation incurred $4.5 million in war debts to the US. Newly elected James K. Polk offered to forgive the debts in return for New Mexico and Upper California, but Mexico refused. In 1846, war was declared in response to a Mexican attack on American troops that President Polk had moved into a disputed zone between the Rio Grande and Nueces River. As US victory grew more certain, dispute arose over how to handle slavery in any newly acquired territory. The **Wilmot Proviso**, though it was never passed, was a large source of contention, as it aimed to prohibit slavery in any territory acquired from Mexico—sowing further seeds of tension between the North and the South. The Mexican-American War ended in 1848 with Mexico agreeing to sell California and its remaining territory north of the Rio Grande.

Review Video: The Mexican-American War
Visit mometrix.com/academy and enter code: 271216

Review Video: Sectional Crisis: The Wilmot Proviso
Visit mometrix.com/academy and enter code: 974842

Popular Sovereignty and the Compromise of 1850

In addition to the pro-slavery and anti-slavery factions, a third group rose, who felt that each individual state should decide whether to allow or permit slavery within its borders. The idea that a state could make its own choices was referred to as **popular sovereignty**.

When California applied to join the union in 1849, the balance of congressional power was again threatened. The **Compromise of 1850** introduced a group of laws meant to bring an end to the conflict:

- California's admittance as a free state
- The outlaw of the slave trade in Washington, DC
- An increase in efforts to capture escaped slaves
- The right of New Mexico and Utah territories to decide individually whether to allow slavery

In spite of these measures, debate raged each time a new state prepared to enter the union.

Gadsden Purchase and the 1853 Post-War Treaty with Mexico

After the Mexican-American war, a **second treaty** in 1853 determined hundreds of miles of America's southwest borders. In 1854, the **Gadsden Purchase** was finalized, providing even more territory to aid in the building of the transcontinental railroad. This purchase added what would eventually become the southernmost regions of Arizona and New Mexico to the growing nation. The modern outline of the United States was by this time nearly complete.

Kansas-Nebraska Act Trigger of Additional Conflict

With the creation of the Kansas and Nebraska territories in 1854, another debate began. Congress allowed popular sovereignty in these territories, but slavery opponents argued that the Missouri Compromise had already made slavery illegal in this region. In Kansas, two separate governments arose, one pro-slavery and one anti-slavery. Conflict between the two factions rose to violence, leading Kansas to gain the nickname of "**Bleeding Kansas**."

Review Video: Sectional Crisis: The Kansas-Nebraska Act
Visit mometrix.com/academy and enter code: 982119

Early Leaders in the Women's Rights Movement

The women's rights movement began in the 1840s, with leaders including Elizabeth Cady Stanton, Sojourner Truth, Ernestine Rose, and Lucretia Mott. In 1869, Elizabeth Cady Stanton and Susan B. Anthony formed the **National Woman Suffrage Association**, fighting for women's right to vote.

In 1848, in Seneca Falls, the first women's rights convention was held, with about 300 attendees. The two-day **Seneca Falls Convention** discussed the rights of women to vote (suffrage) as well as equal treatment in careers, legal proceedings, etc. The convention produced a "Declaration of Sentiments," which outlined a plan for women to attain the rights they deserved. **Frederick Douglass** supported the women's rights movement, as well as the abolition movement. In fact, women's rights and abolition movements often went hand-in-hand during this time period.

Review Video: The Women's Rights Movement in America
Visit mometrix.com/academy and enter code: 987734

Events and Developments that Brought the North and South into Conflict

The conflict between the North and South coalesced around the issue of **slavery**, but other elements contributed to the growing disagreement. Though most farmers in the South worked small farms with little or no slave labor, the huge plantations run by the South's rich depended on slaves or indentured servants to remain profitable. They had also become more dependent on **cotton**, with slave populations growing in concert with the rapid increase in cotton production. In the North, a more diverse agricultural economy and the growth of **industry** made slaves rarer. The **abolitionist movement** grew steadily, with Harriet Beecher Stowe's *Uncle Tom's Cabin* giving many an idea to rally around. A collection of anti-slavery organizations formed, with many actively working to free slaves in the South, often bringing them to the northern states or Canada.

Dred Scott Decision

Abolitionist factions coalesced around the case of **Dred Scott**, using his case to test the country's laws regarding slavery. Scott, a slave, had been taken by his owner from Missouri, which was a slave state. He then traveled to Illinois, a free state, then on to the Minnesota Territory, also free based on the Missouri Compromise. After several years, he returned to Missouri, and his owner subsequently died. Abolitionists took Scott's case to court, stating that Scott was no longer a slave but free, since he had lived in free territory. The case went to the Supreme Court.

The Supreme Court stated that, because Scott, as a slave, was not a US citizen, his time in free states did not change his status. He also did not have the right to sue. In addition, the Court determined that the **Missouri Compromise** was unconstitutional, stating that Congress had overstepped its bounds by outlawing slavery in the territories.

Review Video: The Dred Scott Act
Visit mometrix.com/academy and enter code: 364838

ANTI-SLAVERY ORGANIZATIONS

Five anti-slavery organizations and their significance are:

- **American Colonization Society**—Protestant churches formed this group, aimed at returning black slaves to Africa. Former slaves subsequently formed Liberia, but the colony did not do well, as the region was not well-suited for agriculture.
- **American Anti-Slavery Society**—William Lloyd Garrison, a Quaker, was the major force behind this group and its newspaper, *The Liberator.*
- **Philadelphia Female Anti-Slavery Society**—this women-only group was formed by Margaretta Forten because women were not allowed to join the Anti-Slavery Society formed by her father.
- **Anti-Slavery Convention of American Women**—this group continued meeting even after pro-slavery factions burned down their original meeting place.
- **Female Vigilant Society**—this organization raised funds to help the Underground Railroad, as well as slave refugees.

INCIDENTS AT HARPER'S FERRY AND JOHN BROWN'S ROLE

John Brown, an abolitionist, had participated in several anti-slavery activities, including killing five pro-slavery men in retaliation, after the sacking of Lawrence, Kansas, an anti-slavery town. He and other abolitionists also banded together to pool their funds and build a runaway slave colony.

In 1859, Brown seized a federal arsenal in **Harper's Ferry**, located in what is now West Virginia. Brown intended to seize guns and ammunition and lead a slave rebellion. **Robert E. Lee** captured Brown and 21 followers, who were subsequently tried and hanged. While Northerners took the executions as an indication that the government supported slavery, Southerners were of the opinion that most of the North supported Brown and were, in general, anti-slavery.

PRESIDENTIAL CANDIDATES FOR THE 1860 ELECTION

The 1860 presidential candidates represented four different parties, each with a different opinion on slavery:

- **John Breckinridge**, representing the Southern Democrats, was pro-slavery but urged compromise to preserve the Union.
- **Abraham Lincoln**, of the Republican Party, was anti-slavery.
- **Stephen Douglas**, of the Northern Democrats, felt that the issue should be determined locally, on a state-by-state basis.
- **John Bell**, of the Constitutional Union Party, focused primarily on keeping the Union intact.

In the end, Abraham Lincoln won both the popular and electoral election. Southern states, who had sworn to secede from the Union if Lincoln was elected, did so, led by South Carolina and followed by the rest of the Deep South (Mississippi, Alabama, Georgia, Louisiana, Florida, and Texas). These states established the **Confederate States of America**, with its capital in Montgomery, Alabama.

The president of the CSA was **Jefferson Davis**. Outgoing US President Buchanan claimed that he had no constitutional authority to stop the secession, but upon entering office, Lincoln attempted to maintain control of all Southern forts. This led to the firing on **Ft. Sumter** (SC) by the Confederates. As Lincoln called for aid, the Upper South (Virginia, Arkansas, North Carolina, and Tennessee) seceded as well, and the CSA made Richmond, Virginia its new capital.

Compromises to Save the Union

The US government made a number of compromises in an attempt to preserve the Union after Lincoln's election. The **Crittenden Compromise** extended the line of the Missouri Compromise and promised federal protection of slavery south of that line. The **House of Representatives Compromise** offered an extension of the Missouri Compromise and a Constitutional amendment to protect slavery. The **Virginia Peace Convention** produced an offer to extend the line of the Missouri Compromise and establish that slavery can never be outlawed except by the permission of the owner. Finally, Congress offered $300 for each slave. The South said that this was not enough money, and the North was appalled by the offer, regardless. It became clear that such compromises would not be enough to save the Union.

North vs. South in the Civil War

The Northern states had significant advantages, including:

- **Larger population**—the North consisted of 24 states, while the South had 11.
- **Better transportation and finances**—with railroads primarily in the North, supply chains were much more dependable, as was overseas trade.
- **Raw materials**—the North held the majority of America's gold, as well as iron, copper, and other minerals vital to wartime.

The South's advantages included the following:

- **Better-trained military officers**—many of the Southern officers were West Point trained and had commanded in the Mexican and Indian wars.
- **Familiarity with weapons**—the climate and lifestyle of the South meant most of the people were experienced with both guns and horses. The industrial North had less extensive experience.
- **Defensive position**—the South felt that victory was guaranteed, since they were protecting their own lands, while the North would be invading.
- **Well-defined goals**—the South fought an ideological war to be allowed to govern themselves and preserve their way of life. The North originally fought to preserve the Union and later to free the slaves.

Review Video: American Civil War: North vs. South Overview
Visit mometrix.com/academy and enter code: 370788

Benefit of the Emancipation Proclamation on the Union's Military Strategy

The Emancipation Proclamation, issued by President Lincoln on January 1, 1863, freed all slaves in **Confederate states** that were still in rebellion against the Union. While the original proclamation did not free any slaves in the states actually under Union control, it did set a precedent for the emancipation of slaves as the war progressed.

The **Emancipation Proclamation** worked in the Union's favor, as many freed slaves and other black troops joined the **Union Army**. Almost 200,000 blacks fought in the Union army, and over

10,000 served in the navy. By the end of the war, over 4 million slaves had been freed, and in 1865 slavery was abolished in the **13th amendment** to the Constitution.

Review Video: The Civil War: The Emancipation Proclamation
Visit mometrix.com/academy and enter code: 181778

Major Events of the Civil War

Six major events of the Civil War and their outcomes or significance are:

- The **First Battle of Bull Run** (July 21, 1861)—this was the first major land battle of the war. Observers, expecting to enjoy an entertaining skirmish, set up picnics nearby. Instead, they found themselves witness to a bloodbath. Union forces were defeated, and the battle set the course of the Civil War as long, bloody, and costly.
- The **Capture of Fort Henry** by Ulysses S. Grant—this battle in February of 1862 marked the Union's first major victory.
- The **Battle of Gettysburg** (July 1-3, 1863)—often seen as the turning point of the war, Gettysburg also saw the largest number of casualties of the war, with over 50,000 dead, wounded, or missing. Robert E. Lee was defeated, and the Confederate army, significantly crippled, withdrew.
- The **Overland Campaign** (May and June of 1864)—Grant, now in command of all the Union armies, led this high casualty campaign that eventually positioned the Union for victory.
- **Sherman's March to the Sea**—William Tecumseh Sherman, in May of 1864, conquered Atlanta. He then continued to Savannah, destroying vast amounts of property as he went.
- Following Lee's defeat at the Appomattox Courthouse, General Grant accepted **Lee's surrender** in the home of Wilmer McLean in Appomattox, Virginia on April 9, 1865.

Impact of the Civil War across America

The Civil War impacted various people in America in remarkable ways. The people most affected were likely African Americans, who were at the center of the divide between the North and the South. Many African Americans directly fought in the war on both sides. Those in the Southern states were ultimately freed as a result of the Emancipation Proclamation of 1863. Soldiers in the war saw brutal warfare and faced physical and psychological repercussions of combat. It has long been said about the Civil War that soldiers often knew or were related to the very people they were fighting. This was especially so in states that hosted battles or lied on the borders between Southern and Northern states, such as Virginia and Tennessee. Others affected included women and children who were, in some cases, located fairly near the fights and played roles as suppliers, medics, and activists, leading to some precursors to the women's rights movement. In the reconstruction, economic, political, legal, and emotional fallout had to be dealt with, leading to many decades of repair following the war.

Circumstances of Lincoln's Assassination

The Civil War ended with the surrender of the South on April 9, 1865. Five days later, Lincoln and his wife, Mary, went to the play *Our American Cousin* at the Ford Theater. John Wilkes Booth, who did not know that the war was over, did his part in a plot to help the Confederacy by shooting Lincoln. He was carried from the theater to a nearby house, where he died the next morning. Booth was tracked down and killed by Union soldiers twelve days later.

Review Video: Overview of the American Civil War
Visit mometrix.com/academy and enter code: 239557

Goals of Reconstruction and the Freedmen's Bureau

In the aftermath of the Civil War, the South was left in chaos. From 1865 to 1877, government on all levels worked to help restore order to the South, ensure civil rights to the freed slaves, and bring the Confederate states back into the Union. This became known as the **Reconstruction period**. In 1866, Congress passed the **Reconstruction Acts**, placing former Confederate states under military rule and stating the grounds for readmission into the Union.

The **Freedmen's Bureau** was formed to help freedmen both with basic necessities like food and clothing and also with employment and finding of family members who had been separated during the war. Many in the South felt the Freedmen's Bureau worked to set freed slaves against their former owners. The Bureau was intended to help former slaves become self-sufficient, and to keep them from falling prey to those who would take advantage of them. It eventually closed due to lack of funding and to violence from the **Ku Klux Klan**.

Policies of the Radical and Moderate Republicans

The **Radical Republicans** wished to treat the South quite harshly after the war. **Thaddeus Stevens**, the House Leader, suggested that the Confederate states be treated as if they were territories again, with ten years of military rule and territorial government before they would be readmitted. He also wanted to give all black men the right to vote. Former Confederate soldiers would be required to swear they had never supported the Confederacy (knows as the "Ironclad Oath") in order to be granted full rights as American citizens.

In contrast, the **moderate Republicans** wanted only black men who were literate or who had served as Union troops to be able to vote. All Confederate soldiers except troop leaders would also be able to vote. Before his death, **Lincoln** had favored a more moderate approach to Reconstruction, hoping this approach might bring some states back into the Union before the end of the war.

Phases of Reconstruction

The three phases of Reconstruction are:

- **Presidential Reconstruction**—largely driven by President Andrew Johnson's policies, the presidential phase of Reconstruction was lenient on the South and allowed continued discrimination against and control over blacks.
- **Congressional Reconstruction**—Congress, controlled largely by Radical Republicans, took a different stance, providing a wider range of civil rights for blacks and greater control over Southern government. Congressional Reconstruction is marked by military control of the former Confederate States.
- **Redemption**—gradually, the Confederate states were readmitted into the Union. During this time, white Democrats took over the government of most of the South. In 1877, President Rutherford Hayes withdrew the last federal troops from the South.

Carpetbaggers and Scalawags

The chaos in the South attracted a number of people seeking to fill the power vacuums and take advantage of the economic disruption. **Scalawags** were southern whites who aligned with freedmen to take over local governments. Many in the South who could have filled political offices refused to take the necessary oath required to grant them the right to vote, leaving many opportunities for Scalawags and others. **Carpetbaggers** were Northerners who traveled to the South for various reasons. Some provided assistance, while others sought to make money or to acquire political power during this chaotic period.

Black Codes and the Civil Rights Bill

The Black Codes were proposed to control freed slaves. They would not be allowed to bear arms, assemble, serve on juries, or testify against whites. Schools would be segregated, and unemployed blacks could be arrested and forced to work. The **Civil Rights Act** countered these codes, providing much wider rights for the freed slaves.

Andrew Johnson, who became president after Lincoln's death, supported the Black Codes and vetoed the Civil Rights Act in 1865 and again in 1866. The second time, Congress overrode his veto, and it became law.

Two years later, Congress voted to **impeach** Johnson, the culmination of tensions between Congress and the president. He was tried and came within a single vote of being convicted, but ultimately was acquitted and finished his term in office.

Purpose of the Thirteenth, Fourteenth, and Fifteenth Amendments

The Thirteenth, Fourteenth and Fifteenth Amendments were all passed shortly after the end of the Civil War:

- The **Thirteenth Amendment** was ratified by the states on December 6, 1865. This amendment prohibited slavery in the United States.
- The **Fourteenth Amendment** overturned the Dred Scott decision and was ratified July 9, 1868. American citizenship was redefined: a citizen was any person born or naturalized in the US, with all citizens guaranteed equal legal protection by all states. It also guaranteed citizens of any race the right to file a lawsuit or serve on a jury.
- The **Fifteenth Amendment** was ratified on February 3, 1870. It states that no citizen of the United States can be denied the right to vote based on race, color, or previous status as a slave.

Black Southerners and Segregation

Most Southern Democrats supported **segregation**, or the separation of the races. Although the **Civil Rights Act of 1875** had outlawed segregated restaurants and hotels, among other things, the Supreme Court ruled in 1883 that this act violated the 14th amendment because only states, and not individuals, could be forbidden from segregation. The **Jim Crow laws** were those rules that segregated black people and white people. Although de facto (by custom) segregation had existed in the North for years, the South began to implement segregation de jure (by law). In **Plessy v. Ferguson** (1896), the Supreme Court ruled that accommodations should be "separate but equal." In **Cummings v. Board of Education** (1898), the Supreme Court allowed public schools to be segregated.

Developments in Transportation

As America expanded its borders, it also developed new technology to travel the rapidly growing country. Roads and railroads traversed the nation, with the **Transcontinental Railroad** eventually allowing travel from one coast to the other. Canals and steamboats simplified water travel and made shipping easier and less expensive. The **Erie Canal** (1825) connected the Great Lakes to the Hudson River. Other canals connected other major waterways, further facilitating transportation and the shipment of goods.

Transcontinental Railroad

In 1869, the **Union Pacific Railroad** completed the first section of a planned **transcontinental railroad**. This section went from Omaha, Nebraska to Sacramento, California. Ninety percent of the workers were Chinese, working in very dangerous conditions for very low pay. With the rise of the railroad, products were much more easily transported across the country. While this was positive overall for industry throughout the country, it was often damaging to family farmers, who found themselves paying high shipping costs for smaller supply orders while larger companies received major discounts.

Measures to Limit Immigration in the 19th Century

In 1870, the **Naturalization Act** put limits on US citizenship, allowing full citizenship only to whites and those of African descent. The **Chinese Exclusion Act of 1882** put limits on Chinese immigration. The **Immigration Act of 1882** taxed immigrants, charging 50 cents per person. These funds helped pay administrative costs for regulating immigration. **Ellis Island** opened in 1892 as a processing center for those arriving in New York. The year 1921 saw the **Emergency Quota Act** passed, also known as the **Johnson Quota Act**, which severely limited the number of immigrants allowed into the country.

Agriculture in the 19th Century

Technological Advances in Agricultural Changes

During the mid-1800s, irrigation techniques improved significantly. Advances occurred in cultivation and breeding, as well as fertilizer use and crop rotation. In the Great Plains, also known as the Great American Desert, the dense soil was finally cultivated with steel plows. In 1892, gasoline-powered tractors arrived, and they were widely used by 1900. Other advancements in agriculture's toolset included barbed wire fences, combines, silos, deep-water wells, and the cream separator.

Major Actions that Helped Improve Agriculture

Four major government actions that helped improve US agriculture in the 19th century are:

- The **Department of Agriculture** came into being in 1862, working for the interests of farmers and ranchers across the country.
- The **Morrill Land-Grant Acts** were a series of acts passed between 1862 and 1890, allowing land-grant colleges.
- In conjunction with land-grant colleges, the **Hatch Act of 1887** brought agriculture experiment stations into the picture, helping discover new farming techniques.
- In 1914, the **Smith-Lever Act** provided cooperative programs to help educate people about food, home economics, community development, and agriculture. Related agriculture extension programs helped farmers increase crop production to feed the rapidly growing nation.

Inventors from the 1800s

Major inventors from the 1800s and their inventions include:

- Alexander Graham Bell—the telephone
- Orville and Wilbur Wright—the airplane
- Richard Gatling—the machine gun
- Walter Hunt, Elias Howe, and Isaac Singer—the sewing machine
- Nikola Tesla—alternating current motor
- George Eastman—the Kodak camera
- Thomas Edison—the first commercially practical light bulbs, motion pictures, and the phonograph

- Samuel Morse—the telegraph
- Charles Goodyear—vulcanized rubber
- Cyrus McCormick—the reaper
- George Westinghouse—the transformer, the air brake

This was an active period for invention, with about 700,000 patents registered between 1860 and 1900.

Gilded Age

The time period from the end of the Civil War to the beginning of the First World War is often referred to as the **Gilded Age**, or the **Second Industrial Revolution**. The US was changing from an agricultural-based economy to an **industrial economy**, with rapid growth accompanying the shift. In addition, the country itself was expanding, spreading into the seemingly unlimited west.

This time period saw the beginning of banks, department stores, chain stores, and trusts—all familiar features of the modern-day landscape. Cities also grew rapidly, and large numbers of immigrants arrived in the country, swelling the urban ranks.

Review Video: The Gilded Age: An Overview
Visit mometrix.com/academy and enter code: 684770

Factors Leading to the Development of the Populist Party

A major **recession** struck the United States during the 1890s, with crop prices falling dramatically. **Drought** compounded the problems, leaving many American farmers in crippling debt. The **Farmers' Alliance** formed in 1875, drawing the rural poor into a single political entity.

Recession also affected the more industrial parts of the country. The **Knights of Labor**, formed in 1869 by **Uriah Stephens**, was able to unite workers into a union to protect their rights. Dissatisfied by views espoused by industrialists, the Farmers Alliance and the Knights of Labor, joined to form the **Populist Party**, also known as the People's Party, in 1892. Some of the elements of the party's platform included:

- National currency
- Graduated income tax
- Government ownership of railroads as well as telegraph and telephone systems
- Secret ballots for voting
- Immigration restriction
- Single-term limits for president and vice-president

The Populist Party was in favor of decreasing elitism and making the voice of the common man more easily heard in the political process.

Growth of the Labor Movement Through the Late 19th Century

One of the first large, well-organized strikes occurred in 1892. Called the **Homestead Strike**, it occurred when the Amalgamated Association of Iron and Steel Workers struck against the Carnegie Steel Company. Gunfire ensued, and Carnegie was able to eliminate the plant's union. In 1894, workers in the American Railway Union, led by Eugene Debs, initiated the **Pullman Strike** after the Pullman Palace Car Co. cut their wages by 28 percent. President Grover Cleveland called in troops to break up the strike on the grounds that it interfered with mail delivery. Mary Harris "Mother" Jones organized the **Children's Crusade** to protest child labor. A protest march proceeded to the home of President Theodore Roosevelt in 1903. Jones also worked with the United Mine Workers of America and helped found the **Industrial Workers of the World**.

Panic of 1893

Far from a US-centric event, the **Panic of 1893** was an economic crisis that affected most of the globe. As a response, President Grover Cleveland repealed the **Sherman Silver Purchase Act**, afraid it had caused the downturn rather than boosting the economy as intended. The Panic led to bankruptcies, with banks and railroads going under and factory unemployment rising as high as 25 percent. In the end, the **Republican Party** regained power due to the economic crisis.

Progressive Era

From the 1890s to the end of the First World War, **Progressives** set forth an ideology that drove many levels of society and politics. The Progressives were in favor of workers' rights and safety and wanted measures taken against waste and corruption. They felt science could help improve society and that the government could—and should—provide answers to a variety of social problems. Progressives came from a wide variety of backgrounds but were united in their desire to improve society.

Muckrakers and the Progressive Movement

"Muckrakers" was a term used to identify aggressive investigative journalists who exposed scandals, corruption, and many other wrongs in late 19th-century society. Among these intrepid writers were:

- **Ida Tarbell**—she exposed John D. Rockefeller's Standard Oil Trust.
- **Jacob Riis**—a photographer, he brought the living conditions of the poor in New York to the public's attention.
- **Lincoln Steffens**—he worked to expose political corruption in municipal government.
- **Upton Sinclair**—his book *The Jungle* led to reforms in the meat-packing industry.

Through the work of these journalists, many new policies came into being, including workmen's compensation, child labor laws, and trust-busting.

Dealings with Native Americans Through the End of the 19th Century

America's westward expansion led to conflict and violent confrontations with Native Americans such as the **Battle of Little Bighorn**. In 1876, the American government ordered all Native Americans to relocate to reservations. Lack of compliance led to the **Dawes Act** in 1887, which ordered assimilation rather than separation: Native Americans were offered American citizenship and a piece of their tribal land if they would accept the lot chosen by the government and live on it separately from the tribe. This act remained in effect until 1934. Reformers also forced Native American children to attend **boarding schools**, where they were not allowed to speak their native language and were immersed into a Euro-American culture and religion. Children were often abused in these schools and were indoctrinated to abandon their identity as Native Americans.

In 1890, the massacre at **Wounded Knee**, accompanied by Geronimo's surrender, led the Native Americans to work to preserve their culture rather than fight for their lands.

Review Video: Government Dealings with Native Americans Through 1900
Visit mometrix.com/academy and enter code: 635645

Native Americans in Wartime Through the Beginning of the 20th Century

The **Spanish-American War** (1898) saw a number of Native Americans serving with Teddy Roosevelt in the Rough Riders. Apache scouts accompanied General John J. Pershing to Mexico, hoping to find **Pancho Villa**. More than 17,000 Native Americans were drafted into service for **World War I**, though at the time, they were not considered legal citizens. In 1924, Native Americans were finally granted official citizenship by the **Indian Citizenship Act**.

After decades of relocation, forced assimilation, and genocide, the number of Native Americans in the US has greatly declined. Though many Native Americans have chosen—or have been forced—to assimilate, about 300 reservations exist today, with most of their inhabitants living in abject poverty.

Review Video: Wartime Role of Nativc Americans
Visit mometrix.com/academy and enter code: 419128

Events Leading up to the Spanish-American War

Spain had controlled **Cuba** since the 15th century. Over the centuries, the Spanish had quashed a variety of revolts. In 1886, slavery ended in Cuba, and another revolt was rising.

In the meantime, the US had expressed interest in Cuba, offering Spain $130 million for the island in 1853, during Franklin Pierce's presidency. In 1898, the Cuban revolt was underway. In spite of various factions supporting the Cubans, the US President, William McKinley, refused to recognize the rebellion, preferring negotiation over involvement in war. Then, the *Maine*, a US battleship in Havana Harbor, was blown up, killing 266 crew members. The US declared war two months later, and the war ended with a **Spanish surrender** in less than four months.

American History 1899 to Present

Influence of Big Stick Diplomacy on American Foreign Policy in Latin America

Theodore Roosevelt's famous quote, "Speak softly and carry a big stick," is supposedly of African origins, at least according to Roosevelt. He used this proverb to justify expanded involvement in foreign affairs during his tenure as President. The US military was deployed to protect American interests in **Latin America**. Roosevelt also worked to maintain an equal or greater influence in Latin America than those held by European interests. As a result, the US Navy grew larger, and the US generally became more involved in foreign affairs. Roosevelt felt that if any country was left vulnerable to control by Europe due to economic issues or political instability, the US had not only a right to intervene but was **obligated** to do so. This led to US involvement in Cuba, Nicaragua, Haiti, and the Dominican Republic over several decades leading into the First and Second World Wars.

Importance of the Panama Canal

Initial work began on the **Panama Canal** in 1881, though the idea had been discussed since the 1500s. The canal greatly reduces the length and time needed to sail from one ocean to the other by connecting the Atlantic to the Pacific through the Isthmus of Panama, which joins South America to North America. Before the canal was built, travelers had to sail around the entire perimeter of South America to reach the West Coast of the US. The French began the work after successfully completing the **Suez Canal**, which connected the Mediterranean Sea to the Red Sea. However, due to disease and high expense, the work moved slowly, and after eight years, the company went bankrupt, suspending work. The US purchased the holdings, and the first ship sailed through the canal in 1914. The Panama Canal was constructed as a lock-and-lake canal, with ships lifted on locks to travel from one lake to another over the rugged, mountainous terrain. In order to maintain control of the Canal Zone, the US assisted Panama in its battle for independence from **Colombia**.

Taft's Dollar Diplomacy vs. Roosevelt's Diplomatic Theories

During William Howard Taft's presidency, Taft instituted "**Dollar Diplomacy**." This approach was America's effort to influence Latin America and East Asia through economic rather than military means. Taft saw past efforts in these areas to be political and warlike, while his efforts focused on peaceful economic goals. His justification of the policy was to protect the **Panama Canal**, which was vital to US trade interests.

In spite of Taft's assurance that Dollar Diplomacy was a peaceful approach, many interventions proved violent. During Latin American revolts, such as those in **Nicaragua**, the US sent troops to settle the revolutions. Afterward, bankers moved in to help support the new leaders through loans. Dollar Diplomacy continued until 1913, when Woodrow Wilson was elected president.

Growth of Civil Rights for African Americans

Marcus Garvey founded the **Universal Negro Improvement Association and African Communities League (UNIA-ACL)**, which became a large and active organization focused on building black nationalism. In 1909, the **National Association for the Advancement of Colored People (NAACP)** came into being, working to defeat Jim Crow laws. The NAACP also helped prevent racial segregation from becoming federal law, fought against lynchings, helped black soldiers in WWI become officers, and helped defend the Scottsboro Boys, who were unjustly accused of rape.

Wilson's Approach to International Diplomacy

Turning away from Taft's "Dollar Diplomacy," Wilson instituted a foreign policy he referred to as "**moral diplomacy**." This approach still influences American foreign policy today.

Wilson felt that **representative government and democracy** in all countries would lead to worldwide stability. Democratic governments, he felt, would be less likely to threaten American interests. He also saw the US and Great Britain as the great role models in this area, as well as champions of world peace and self-government. Free trade and international commerce would allow the US to speak out regarding world events.

Main elements of Wilson's policies included:

- Maintaining a strong military
- Promoting democracy throughout the world
- Expanding international trade to boost the American economy

The Sixteenth, Seventeenth, Eighteenth, and Nineteenth Amendments

The early 20th century saw several amendments made to the US Constitution:

- The **Sixteenth Amendment** (1913) established a federal income tax.
- The **Seventeenth Amendment** (1913) allowed popular election of senators.
- The **Eighteenth Amendment** (1919) prohibited the sale, production, and transportation of alcohol. This amendment was later repealed by the Twenty-first Amendment.
- The **Nineteenth Amendment** (1920) gave women the right to vote.

These amendments largely grew out of the Progressive Era, as many citizens worked to improve American society.

Goals of the Anti-Defamation League

In 1913, the Anti-Defamation League was formed to prevent anti-Semitic behavior and practices. Its actions also worked to prevent all forms of racism and to prevent individuals from being discriminated against for any reason involving their race. They spoke against the Ku Klux Klan, as well as other racist or anti-Semitic organizations. This organization still works to fight discrimination against all minorities.

Role of the Federal Trade Commission in Eliminating Trusts

Muckrakers such as Ida Tarbell and Lincoln Steffens brought to light the damaging trend of trusts—huge corporations working to monopolize areas of commerce so they could control prices and distribution. The **Sherman Antitrust Act** and the **Clayton Antitrust Act** set out guidelines for competition among corporations and set out to eliminate these trusts. The **Federal Trade Commission** was formed in 1914 in order to enforce antitrust measures and ensure that companies were operated fairly and did not create controlling monopolies.

Major Events of World War I

World War I occurred from 1914 to 1918 and was fought largely in Europe. The rise in **nationalism** at the beginning of the 20th century helped contribute to the possibility of war. There was also some conflict between the **imperialist** (France, Britain, and the US) and the **non-imperialist** (Germany, Italy) nations. Many large nations were seeking economic expansion outside of their own borders, and the competition for foreign markets was intense. There was also a complex system of entangling alliances; many countries were involved in several different alliances at the same time. The spark for World War I, though, was the assassination of **Archduke Franz Ferdinand**, heir to the throne of Austria-Hungary, in April of 1914 by a Serbian nationalist. When Emperor Franz Joseph declared war on Serbia, it set off a chain reaction that involved virtually every nation in Europe. At the beginning of the conflict, Woodrow Wilson declared the US neutral. Eventually, however, the US joined the war. Major events influencing US involvement included:

- **Sinking of the *Lusitania***—the British passenger liner RMS *Lusitania* was sunk by a German U-boat in 1915. Among the 1,000 civilian victims were over 100 American citizens. Outraged by this act, many Americans began to push for US involvement in the war, using the *Lusitania* as a rallying cry.
- **German U-boat aggression**—Wilson continued to keep the US out of the war, using as his 1916 reelection slogan, "He kept us out of war." While he continued to work toward an end of the war, German U-boats began to indiscriminately attack American and Canadian merchant ships carrying supplies to Germany's enemies in Europe.
- **Zimmerman Telegram** —the final event that brought the US into World War I was the interception of the Zimmerman Telegram (also known as the Zimmerman Note) on January 17th, 1917. In this telegram, Germany proposed forming an alliance with Mexico if the US entered the war.

Efforts in the US During World War I Supporting the War Effort

American **railroads** came under government control in December 1917. The widespread system was consolidated into a single system, with each region assigned a director. This greatly increased the efficiency of the railroad system, allowing the railroads to supply both domestic and military needs. Control returned to private ownership in 1920. In 1918, **telegraph, telephone, and cable services** also came under Federal control, to be returned to private management the next year. The **American Red Cross** supported the war effort by knitting clothes for Army and Navy troops. They also helped supply hospital and refugee clothing and surgical dressings. Over 8 million people participated in this effort. To generate wartime funds, the US government sold **Liberty Bonds**. In four issues, they sold nearly $25 billion—more than one-fifth of Americans purchased them. After the war, a fifth bond drive was held but sold "**Victory Liberty Bonds**."

Review Video: WWI Overview
Visit mometrix.com/academy and enter code: 659767

Influence of Wilson's Fourteen Points on Final Peace Treaties

President Woodrow Wilson proposed **Fourteen Points** as the basis for a peace settlement to end the war. Presented to the US Congress in January 1918, the Fourteen Points included:

- Five points outlining **general ideals**
- Eight points to resolve **immediate problems** of political and territorial nature
- One point proposing an **organization of nations** (the League of Nations) with the intent of maintaining world peace

In November of that same year, Germany agreed to an **armistice**, assuming the final treaty would be based on the Fourteen Points. However, during the peace conference in Paris 1919, there was much disagreement, leading to a final agreement that punished Germany and the other Central Powers much more than originally intended. Henry Cabot Lodge, who had become the Foreign Relations Committee chairman in 1918, wanted an unconditional surrender from Germany and was concerned about the article in the **Treaty of Versailles** that gave the League of Nations power to declare war without a vote from the US Congress. A **League of Nations** was included in the Treaty of Versailles at Wilson's insistence. The Senate rejected the Treaty of Versailles, and in the end, Wilson refused to concede to Lodge's demands. As a result, the US did not join the League of Nations.

Origins of the Red Scare

World War I created many jobs, but after the war ended, these jobs disappeared, leaving many unemployed. In the wake of these employment changes, the **International Workers of the World** and the **Socialist Party**, headed by Eugene Debs, became more and more visible. Workers initiated strikes in an attempt to regain the favorable working conditions that had been put into place before the war. Unfortunately, many of these strikes became violent, and the actions were blamed on "Reds," or Communists, for trying to spread their views into America. With the recent Bolshevik Revolution in Russia, many Americans feared a similar revolution might occur in the US. The **Red Scare** ensued, with many individuals jailed for supposedly holding communist, anarchist, or socialist beliefs.

Major Changes and Events that Took Place in America During the 1920s

The post-war 1920s saw many Americans moving from the farm to the city, with growing prosperity in the US. The **Roaring Twenties**, or the **Jazz Age**, was driven largely by growth in the automobile and entertainment industries. Individuals like Charles Lindbergh, the first aviator to make a solo flight across the Atlantic Ocean, added to the American admiration of individual accomplishment. Telephone lines, distribution of electricity, highways, the radio, and other inventions brought great changes to everyday life.

Review Video: 1920's
Visit mometrix.com/academy and enter code: 124996

Prohibition

The Eighteenth Amendment was ratified by most states in 1919, making the manufacture, sale, transportation, importation, and exportation of alcohol illegal; however, this change was not enforced with much success. Instead of curbing the production and consumption of alcohol, Prohibition led to the creation of a large, illegal alcohol market dominated by organized crime. Criminal organizations, like the Mafia crime syndicate, grew massively in power and influence during the 1920s and 1930s by cornering the market on the production, distribution, and sale of alcohol. Americans continued to drink alcohol in speakeasies—hidden, illegal drinking establishments. The huge illegal market for alcohol contributed to increased crime and unregulated, sometimes dangerous, alcohol.

Major Cultural Movements of the 1920s Influenced by African Americans

The **Harlem Renaissance** saw a number of African-American artists settling in Harlem in New York. This community produced a number of well-known artists and writers, including Langston Hughes, Nella Larsen, Zora Neale Hurston, Claude McKay, Countee Cullen, and Jean Toomer. The growth of jazz, also largely driven by African Americans, defined the **Jazz Age**. Its unconventional, improvisational style matched the growing sense of optimism and exploration of the decade. Originating as an offshoot of the blues, jazz began in New Orleans. Some significant jazz musicians were Duke Ellington, Louis Armstrong, and Jelly Roll Morton. **Big Band** and **Swing Jazz** also developed in the 1920s. Well-known musicians of this movement included Bing Crosby, Frank Sinatra, Count Basie, Benny Goodman, Billie Holiday, Ella Fitzgerald, and The Dorsey Brothers.

American Civil Liberties Union

The American Civil Liberties Union (**ACLU**), founded in 1920, grew from the American Union Against Militarism. The ACLU helped conscientious objectors avoid going to war during WWI, and also helped those being prosecuted under the **Espionage Act** (1917) and the **Sedition Act** (1918), many of whom were immigrants. Their major goals were to protect immigrants and other citizens who were threatened with prosecution for their political beliefs, and to support labor unions, which were also under threat by the government during the Red Scare.

Womens' Suffrage

The Nineteenth Amendment gave **women the right to vote**. This amendment was proposed on June 4, 1919, and was ratified on August 18, 1920. An amendment to give women the right to vote was first introduced in Congress in 1878, but it failed to pass. For the next four decades, the amendment was reintroduced in every session of Congress but was defeated each time. The involvement of women in the war effort during World War I spawned increased support for women's suffrage. Finally, in 1918, the House of Representatives approved the amendment to grant women suffrage, but the Senate defeated it. In 1919, the Senate also passed the amendment and sent it to the states for approval, where it was ratified in 1920.

Provisions and Importance of the National Origins Act of 1924

The National Origins Act (Johnson-Reed Act) placed limitations on **immigration**. The number of immigrants allowed into the US was based on the population of each nationality of immigrants who were living in the country in 1890. Only two percent of each nationality's 1890 population numbers were allowed to immigrate. This led to great disparities between immigrants from various nations, and Asian immigration was not allowed at all. Some of the impetus behind the Johnson-Reed Act came as a result of paranoia following the **Russian Revolution**. Fear of communist influences in the US led to a general fear of immigrants.

Ku Klux Klan

In 1866, Confederate Army veterans came together to fight against Reconstruction in the South, forming a group called the **Ku Klux Klan (KKK)**. With white supremacist beliefs, including anti-Semitism, nativism, anti-Catholicism, and overt racism, this organization relied heavily on violence to get its message across. In 1915, they grew again in power, using a film called *The Birth of a Nation*, by D.W. Griffith, to spread their ideas. In the 1920s, the reach of the KKK spread far into the north and midwest, and members controlled a number of state governments. Its membership and power began to decline during the Great Depression but experienced a resurgence later.

The Great Depression

The **Great Depression** was the largest economic downturn in the history of the United States. It began in 1929 with the stock market crash and ended around 1939. The Great Depression grew out of several factors that had developed over the previous years, including:

- Growing economic disparity between the rich and middle classes, with the rich amassing wealth much more quickly than the lower classes
- Disparity in economic distribution in industries
- Growing use of credit, leading to an inflated demand for some goods
- Government support of new industries rather than agriculture
- Risky stock market investments, leading to the stock market crash

Additional factors contributing to the Depression also included the **Labor Day Hurricane** in the Florida Keys (1935) and the **Great Hurricane of 1938** in New England, along with the **Dust Bowl** in the Great Plains, which destroyed crops and resulted in the displacement of as many as 2.5 million people.

Review Video: Causes of the Great Depression
Visit mometrix.com/academy and enter code: 635912

The Dust Bowl

The Dust Bowl (1930-1941) was a period of American history characterized by a high incidence of dust storms in the Great Plains region. The instability of the world agriculture market during World War I led to overproduction in the 1920s. Even lands previously considered unsuitable for agricultural use were leveled and developed. This excessive activity devastated the Great Plains, eliminating the natural vegetation that could have prevented the massive soil movement that occurred during the drought and strong winds of the 1930s, and resulted in widespread crop failure. In turn, the Dust Bowl led to millions of people being displaced from their homes and hundreds of thousands migrating to California in search of work and better living conditions. On their journeys, however, these migrants faced poor conditions, starvation, and dehydration. Even when they arrived in California, many of them struggled to find work. The work that was available was often hard labor, like picking cotton. Migrants also faced hostility and even phyisical violence from locals. They were often forced to live in roadside camps, which were sometimes the target of arson.

Franklin D. Roosevelt's Election and New Deal

Franklin D. Roosevelt was elected president in 1932 with his promise of a "**New Deal**" for Americans. His goals were to provide government work programs to provide jobs, wages, and relief to numerous workers throughout the beleaguered US. Congress gave Roosevelt almost free rein to produce relief legislation. The goals of this legislation were:

- **Relief**—creating jobs for the high numbers of unemployed
- **Recovery**—stimulating the economy through the National Recovery Administration
- **Reform**—passing legislation to prevent future, similar economic crashes

The Roosevelt Administration also passed legislation regarding ecological issues, including the Soil Conservation Service, aimed at preventing another Dust Bowl.

Roosevelt's Alphabet Organizations

So-called "alphabet organizations" set up during Roosevelt's administration included:

- **Civilian Conservation Corps** (CCC)—provided jobs in the forestry service
- **Agricultural Adjustment Administration** (AAA)—increased agricultural income by adjusting both production and prices
- **Tennessee Valley Authority** (TVA)—organized projects to build dams in the Tennessee River for flood control and production of electricity, resulting in increased productivity for industries in the area, and easier navigation of the Tennessee River
- **Public Works Administration** (PWA) and Civil Works Administration (CWA)—provided a multitude of jobs, initiating over 34,000 projects
- **Works Progress Administration** (WPA)—helped unemployed persons to secure employment on government work projects or elsewhere

Actions Taken During the Roosevelt Administration to Prevent Future Crashes

The Roosevelt administration passed several laws and established several institutions to initiate the "reform" portion of the New Deal, including:

- **Glass-Steagall Act**—separated investment from commercial banking
- **Securities Exchange Commission (SEC)**—helped regulate Wall Street investment practices, making them less dangerous to the overall economy
- **Wagner Act**—provided worker and union rights to improve relations between employees and employers
- **Social Security Act of 1935**—provided pensions as well as unemployment insurance

Other actions focused on insuring bank deposits and adjusting the value of American currency. Most of these regulatory agencies and government policies and programs still exist today.

Major Regulations Regarding Labor During the Great Depression

Three major regulations regarding labor that were passed after the Great Depression are:

- **Davis-Bacon Act** (1931)—provided fair compensation for contractors and subcontractors.
- The **Wagner Act** (1935)—also known as the National Labor Relations Act, it established that unions were legal, protected members of unions, and required collective bargaining. This act was later amended by the Taft-Hartley Act of 1947 and the Landrum-Griffin Act of 1959, which further clarified certain elements.
- **Walsh-Healey Act** (1936)—established a minimum wage, child labor laws, safety standards, and overtime pay.

World War II

America's Introduction to WWII

After the First World War, the US became obsessed with isolating itself from foreign conflicts. The **Nye Committee** studied the war and determined that it had been fought for financial reasons and could have been avoided. Isolationist parties achieved some popularity during this period, including the **America First Committee**, led by Charles Lindbergh, and **SOS** (Stop Organized Slaughter). The **Neutrality Laws** of 1935-7 declared that the US could not sell weapons to another country in a time of war and that US citizens could not travel on the ships of a nation at war. In 1937, FDR delivered the **Quarantine Speech**, in which he asserted that the Nazi "disease" must be contained. Finally, after conflict in Europe had escalated considerably, FDR declared that the US needed to help Britain and be an "arsenal of democracy in the world." The **Neutrality Act of 1940** made it legal for the US to sell weapons on a cash and carry basis. In August of 1941, FDR and Churchill drew up the **Atlantic Charter**, which vowed to destroy Nazism, protect the right of self-determination, and create a World Peace Organization.

Buildup to the Attack on Pearl Harbor

A number of events had created a stormy relationship between the US and Japan long before the invasion of Pearl Harbor, but the conflict reached a boiling point after President Roosevelt froze all Japanese assets in the US and cut Japan off from US oil and steel. America also had a cordial relationship at this time with Japan's longtime rival, China. The Japanese launched surprise attacks both on the American naval base at **Pearl Harbor** and on the **Philippines**, where they hoped to secure some oil.

US Involvement in WWII Concerning Europe and Africa

After the Japanese attack on Pearl Harbor in 1941, the US declared **war** on Japan, after which Germany declared war on the US. Before going after Japan, however, the US first attacked Germany; this was done because the US underestimated Japan industrially and militarily, and because the US feared Britain was on the verge of defeat. **Operation Overlord**, the Allied invasion of the European continent at Normandy, was led in part by General **Dwight D. Eisenhower**. The American generals Omar Bradley and George Patton took part in the **Allied Operation Torch**, aimed at taking back North Africa. At the **Battle of the Bulge**, in Belgium, the Germans tried to break the Allied lines, but were unsuccessful, in part because of the heroism of American soldiers.

US Involvement in WWII Concerning Asia and the Pacific

The US strategy for controlling the Pacific was known as "island hopping." In the **Coral Sea Battle of 1942**, Americans stopped the Japanese from taking Australia and New Guinea. In the same year, the **Doolittle raids** of Japanese naval bases boosted American morale. In the **Battle of Midway** (1942), the US sunk four Japanese aircraft carriers. In the **Battle of Leyte Gulf**, General Douglas MacArthur took back the Philippines and also took control of Iwo Jima and Okinawa. During this period, a team of American scientists led by Robert Oppenheimer was developing the **atomic bomb** in Los Alamos, New Mexico. Japan was warned several times by President Truman that the bomb would be used if they did not surrender. Surely enough, Americans dropped atomic bombs on **Hiroshima** on August 6, 1945, and on **Nagasaki** three days later. Japanese leaders surrendered aboard the USS Missouri on August 15, 1945.

The Holocaust is the name given to the systematic killing of Jews, Gypsies, homosexuals, and others by the Nazis. **Anti-Semitism** had existed in Europe for a long time, but the Nazis gave it renewed emphasis and, after making numerous false claims about Jews, began persecuting them upon Hitler's rise to power in 1933. Jews were disenfranchised, forced into ghettos, had their property taken, and were finally sent to work and be killed in **concentration camps**. Approximately 6 million Jews were killed during the **Holocaust**. As the situation for the Germans became more dire in the Second World War, Hitler sought to implement what he called the "final solution," in which hundreds of thousands were killed just before the fall of Nazi Germany.

Interventionist and Isolationist Approaches in World War II

When war broke out in Europe in 1939, President Roosevelt stated that the US would remain **neutral**. However, his overall approach was considered "**interventionist**," as he was willing to provide aid to the Allies without actually entering the conflict. Thus, the US supplied a wide variety of war materials to the Allied nations in the early years of the war.

Isolationists believed the US should not provide any aid to the Allies, including supplies. They felt Roosevelt, by assisting the Allies, was leading the US into a war for which it was not prepared. Led by Charles Lindbergh, the Isolationists believed that any involvement in the European conflict endangered the US by weakening its national defense.

Sequence of Events that Led the US to Declare War and Enter World War II

In 1937, Japan invaded China, prompting the US to eventually halt exports to Japan. Roosevelt also did not allow Japanese interests to withdraw money held in US banks. In 1941, **General Tojo** rose to power as the Japanese prime minister. Recognizing America's ability to bring a halt to Japan's expansion, he authorized the bombing of **Pearl Harbor** on December 7. The US responded by declaring war on Japan. Partially because of the **Tripartite Pact** among the Axis Powers, Germany and Italy then declared war on the US, later followed by Bulgaria, Hungary, and other Axis nations.

Review Video: World War II Overview
Visit mometrix.com/academy and enter code: 759402

Occurrences of World War II that Led to the Surrender of Germany

In 1941, **Hitler** violated the non-aggression pact he had signed with Stalin two years earlier by invading the USSR. **Stalin** then joined the **Allies**. Stalin, Roosevelt, and Winston Churchill planned to defeat Germany first, then Japan, bringing the war to an end.

In 1942-1943, the Allies drove **Axis** forces out of Africa. In addition, the Germans were soundly defeated at Stalingrad.

The **Italian Campaign** involved Allied operations in Italy between July 1943 and May 1945, including Italy's liberation. On June 6, 1944, known as **D-Day**, the Allies invaded France at Normandy. Soviet troops moved on the eastern front at the same time, driving German forces back. By April 25, 1945, Berlin was surrounded by Soviet troops. On May 7, Germany surrendered.

Major Events of World War II that Led to the Surrender of Japan

War continued with **Japan** after Germany's surrender. Japanese forces had taken a large portion of Southeast Asia and the Western Pacific, all the way to the Aleutian Islands in Alaska. **General Doolittle** bombed several Japanese cities while American troops scored a victory at Midway. Additional fighting in the Battle of the Coral Sea further weakened Japan's position. As a final blow, the US dropped two **atomic bombs** on Japan, one on Hiroshima and the other on Nagasaki. This was the first time atomic bombs had been used in warfare, and the devastation was horrific and demoralizing. Japan surrendered on September 2, 1945, which became **V-J Day** in the US.

The 442nd Regimental Combat Team, Tuskegee Airmen, and Navajo Code Talkers

The 442nd Regimental Combat Team consisted of Japanese-Americans fighting in Europe for the US. The most highly decorated unit per member in US history, they suffered a 93% casualty rate during the war. The **Tuskegee Airmen** were African American aviators, the first black Americans allowed to fly for the military. In spite of being ineligible to become official navy pilots, they flew over 15,000 missions and were highly decorated. The **Navajo Code Talkers** were native Navajo who used their traditional language to transmit information among Allied forces. Because Navajo is a highly-complex and unwritten language and not simply a code, the Axis powers were never able to translate it. The use of Navajo Code Talkers to transmit information was instrumental in the taking of Iwo Jima and other major victories of the war.

Circumstances and Opportunities for Women During World War II

Women served widely in the military during WWII, working in numerous positions, including the **Flight Nurses Corps**. Women also moved into the workforce while men were overseas, leading to over 19 million women in the US workforce by 1944. **Rosie the Riveter** stood as a symbol of these women and a means of recruiting others to take needed positions. Women, as well as their families left behind during wartime, also grew **Victory Gardens** to help provide food.

Japanese-American Internment During World War II

Following the attack on Pearl Harbor, the American government began to suspect that people of Japanese ancestry in America may be operating as spies for Japan, though there was little evidence for this. Just a couple of months after the attack, President Franklin D. Roosevelt signed Executive Order 9066, which allowed the government to declare Military Exclusion Zones for the purpose of national security. This made it legal for the military to remove people or other perceived threats from these exclusion zones. As a result, over 100,000 people of Japanese ancestry were removed from their homes in these areas and placed into internment camps. These camps were hastily built and offered poor living conditions. Children interned in these camps did not have access to a full education, and many Japanese-Americans lost their businesses and homes as a result of their internment.

In **Korematsu v. US** (1944), the Supreme Court ruled that the internment camps were legal, but in **ex parte Endo** (1944), the Court adjusted its decision to state that the US could only intern those whose disloyalty could be proven. Japanese internment ended in 1945, but the effects of internment on Japanese-Americans endured.

Importance of the Atomic Bomb During World War II

The atomic bomb, developed during WWII, was the most powerful bomb ever invented. A single bomb, carried by a single plane, held enough power to destroy an entire city. This devastating effect was demonstrated with the bombing of **Hiroshima** and **Nagasaki** in 1945 in what later became a controversial move, but ended the war. The bombings resulted in as many as 150,000 immediate deaths and many more as time passed after the bombings, mostly due to **radiation poisoning**.

Whatever the arguments against the use of "The Bomb," the post-WWII era saw many countries develop similar weapons to match the newly expanded military power of the US. The impact of those developments and use of nuclear weapons continues to haunt international relations today.

Importance of the Yalta Conference and the Potsdam Conference

In February 1945, Joseph Stalin, Franklin D. Roosevelt, and Winston Churchill met in Yalta to discuss the post-war treatment of the **Axis nations**, particularly Germany. Though Germany had not yet surrendered, its defeat was imminent. After Germany's official surrender, Joseph Stalin,

Harry Truman (Roosevelt's successor), and Clement Attlee (replacing Churchill partway through the conference) met to formalize those plans. This meeting was called the **Potsdam Conference**. Basic provisions of these agreements included:

- Dividing Germany and Berlin into four zones of occupation
- Demilitarization of Germany
- Poland remaining under Soviet control
- Outlawing the Nazi Party
- Trials for Nazi leaders
- Relocation of numerous German citizens
- The USSR joining the United Nations, established in 1945
- Establishment of the United Nations Security Council, consisting of the US, the UK, the USSR, China, and France

Agreements Made with Post-War Japan

General Douglas MacArthur led the American **military occupation of Japan** after the country surrendered. The goals of the US occupation included removing Japan's military and making the country a democracy. A 1947 constitution removed power from the emperor and gave it to the people, as well as granting voting rights to women. Japan was no longer allowed to declare war, and a group of 28 government officials were tried for war crimes. In 1951, the US finally signed a peace treaty with Japan. This treaty allowed Japan to rearm itself for purposes of self-defense but stripped the country of the empire it had built overseas.

US Treatment of Immigrants During and After World War II

In 1940, the US passed the **Alien Registration Act**, which required all aliens older than fourteen to be fingerprinted and registered. They were also required to report changes of address within five days.

Tension between whites and Japanese immigrants in **California**, which had been building since the beginning of the century, came to a head with the bombing of **Pearl Harbor** in 1941. Believing that even those Japanese living in the US were likely to be loyal to their native country, the president ordered numerous Japanese to be arrested on suspicion of subversive action and isolated in exclusion zones known as **War Relocation Camps**. Approximately 120,000 Japanese-Americans, two-thirds of them US citizens, were sent to these camps during the war.

General State of the US After World War II

Following WWII, the US became the strongest political power in the world, becoming a major player in world affairs and foreign policies. The US determined to stop the spread of **communism**, having named itself the "**arsenal of democracy**" during the war. In addition, America emerged with a greater sense of itself as a single, integrated nation, with many regional and economic differences diminished. The government worked for greater equality, and the growth of communications increased contact among different areas of the country. Both the aftermath of the Great Depression and the necessities of WWII had given the government greater **control** over various institutions as well as the economy. This also meant that the American government took on greater responsibility for the well-being of its citizens, both in the domestic arena, such as providing basic needs, and in protecting them from foreign threats. This increased role of providing basic necessities for all Americans has been criticized by some as "**the welfare state**."

FEAR OF COMMUNISM FOLLOWING WORLD WAR II

After World War II, America became greatly concerned with the spread of communism, which was being propagated mainly by the Soviet Union and the communist party in China. A series of policies in America, Western Europe, and the Soviet Union brought the anti-communist and communist groups ever closer to open conflict. As these tensions grew in the international community, Americans became increasingly paranoid about the spread of **Communism**. There were numerous investigations aimed at weeding Communist spies out of the government, and two people, Julius and Ethel Rosenberg, were executed for spying. The leader of much of this was Senator **Joseph McCarthy**, who was famous for promoting and prolonging the "**Red Scare**" as the often-termed witch-hunt for communists in the government was known (Soviet communications released after the fall of the Soviet Union confirmed the vast majority of his accusations). The tide of anti-communism extended into a general disapproval of organized labor. The **Taft-Hartley Act** restricted the ability of labor unions markedly. In order to survive, the nation's two largest labor unions combined, forming the **AFL-CIO**.

US POLICY TOWARD IMMIGRANTS AFTER WORLD WAR II

Prior to WWII, the US had been limiting **immigration** for several decades. After WWII, policy shifted slightly to accommodate political refugees from Europe and elsewhere. So many people were displaced by the war that in 1946, the UN formed the **International Refugee Organization** to deal with the problem. In 1948, the US Congress passed the **Displaced Persons Act**, which allowed over 400,000 European refugees to enter the US, most of them concentration camp survivors and refugees from Eastern Europe.

In 1952, the **United States Escapee Program (USEP)** increased the quotas, allowing refugees from communist Europe to enter the US, as did the **Refugee Relief Act**, passed in 1953. At the same time, however, the **Internal Security Act of 1950** allowed deportation of declared communists, and Asians were subjected to a quota based on race, rather than country of origin. Later changes included:

- **Migration and Refugee Assistance Act** (1962)—provided aid for refugees in need
- **Immigration and Nationality Act** (1965)—ended quotas based on nation of origin
- **Immigration Reform and Control Act** (1986)—prohibited the hiring of illegal immigrants but also granted amnesty to about three million illegals already in the country

ACCOMPLISHMENTS OF HARRY S. TRUMAN

Harry S. Truman took over the presidency from Franklin D. Roosevelt near the end of WWII. He made the final decision to drop atomic bombs on Japan and played a major role in the final decisions regarding the treatment of post-war Germany. On the domestic front, Truman initiated a 21-point plan known as the **Fair Deal**. This plan expanded Social Security, provided public housing, and made the Fair Employment Practice Committee permanent. Truman helped support Greece and Turkey (which were under threat from the USSR), supported South Korea against communist North Korea, and helped with recovery in Western Europe. He also participated in the formation of **NATO**, the North Atlantic Treaty Organization.

EVENTS AND IMPORTANCE OF THE KOREAN WAR

The Korean War began in 1950 and ended in 1953. For the first time in history, a world organization—the **United Nations**—played a military role in a war. North Korea sent communist troops into South Korea, seeking to bring the entire country under communist control. The UN sent out a call to member nations, asking them to support South Korea. Truman sent troops, as did many other UN member nations. The war ended three years later with a **truce** rather than a peace treaty, and Korea remains divided at the **38th parallel north**, with communist rule remaining in the North and a democratic government ruling the South.

Effects of US Cold War Foreign Policy Acts on the International Relationships

The following are US Cold War foreign policy acts and how they affected international relationships, especially between the US and the Soviet Union:

- **Marshall Plan**—this sent aid to war-torn Europe after WWII, largely focusing on preventing the spread of communism.
- **Containment Policy**—proposed by George F. Kennan, the containment policy focused on containing the spread of Soviet communism.
- **Truman Doctrine**—Harry S. Truman stated that the US would provide both economic and military support to any country threatened by Soviet takeover.
- **National Security Act**—passed in 1947, this act reorganized the government's military departments into the Department of Defense and created the Central Intelligence Agency and the National Security Council.

The combination of these acts led to the **Cold War**, with Soviet communists attempting to spread their influence and the US and other countries trying to contain or stop this spread.

Accomplishments of Dwight D. Eisenhower

Eisenhower carried out a middle-of-the-road foreign policy and brought the US several steps forward in equal rights. He worked to minimize tensions during the Cold War and negotiated a peace treaty with Russia after the death of Stalin. He enforced desegregation by sending troops to Little Rock Central High School in Arkansas, as well as ordering the desegregation of the military. Organizations formed during his administration included the Department of Health, Education, and Welfare, and the National Aeronautics and Space Administration (NASA).

Effect of the Arms Race on Post WWII International Relations

After World War II, major nations, particularly the US and USSR, rushed to develop highly advanced weapons systems such as the **atomic bomb** and later the **hydrogen bomb**. These countries seemed determined to outpace each other with the development of numerous, deadly weapons. These weapons were expensive and extremely dangerous, and it is possible that the war between US and Soviet interests remained "cold" due to the fear that one side or the other would use these powerful weapons.

Technological Advances that Occurred Throughout the 1900s

Numerous technological advances throughout the 1900s led to more effective treatment of diseases, more efficient communication and transportation, and new means of generating power. Advances in **medicine** increased the human lifespan in developed countries, and near-instantaneous **communication** opened up a myriad of possibilities. Some of these advances include:

- Discovery of penicillin (1928)
- Supersonic air travel (1947)
- Nuclear power plants (1951)
- Orbital satellite leading to manned space flight (Sputnik, 1957)
- First man on the moon (1969)

NATO, Warsaw Pact, and the Berlin Wall

NATO, the **North Atlantic Treaty Organization**, came into being in 1949. It essentially amounted to an agreement among the US and Western European countries that an attack on any one of these countries was to be considered an attack against the entire group. Under the influence of the Soviet Union, the Eastern European countries of the USSR, Bulgaria, East Germany, Poland, Romania, Albania, Hungary, and Czechoslovakia responded with the **Warsaw Pact**, which created a similar agreement among those nations. In 1961, a wall was built to separate communist East Berlin from democratic West Berlin. This was a literal representation of the "**Iron Curtain**" that separated the democratic and communist countries throughout the world.

Presidency of John F. Kennedy

Although his term was cut short by his assassination, **JFK** instituted economic programs that led to a period of continuous expansion in the US unmatched since before WWII. He formed the Alliance for Progress and the Peace Corps, organizations intended to help developing nations. He also oversaw the passage of new civil rights legislation and drafted plans to attack poverty and its causes, along with support of the arts. Kennedy's presidency ended when he was assassinated by **Lee Harvey Oswald** in 1963.

Events of the Cuban Missile Crisis

The Cuban Missile Crisis occurred in 1962, during John F. Kennedy's presidency. Russian Premier **Nikita Khrushchev** decided to place nuclear missiles in **Cuba** to protect the island from invasion by the US. An American U-2 plane flying over the island photographed the missile bases as they were being built. Tensions rose, with the US concerned about nuclear missiles so close to its shores, and the USSR concerned about American missiles that had been placed in **Turkey**. Eventually, the missile sites were removed, and a US naval blockade turned back Soviet ships carrying missiles to Cuba. During negotiations, the US agreed to remove their missiles from Turkey and agreed to sell surplus wheat to the USSR. A telephone hotline between Moscow and Washington was set up to allow instant communication between the two heads of state to prevent similar incidents in the future.

Accomplishments of the Lyndon B. Johnson Presidency

Kennedy's vice president, **Lyndon Johnson**, assumed the presidency after Kennedy's **assassination**. He supported civil rights bills, tax cuts, and other wide-reaching legislation that Kennedy had also supported. Johnson saw America as a "**Great Society**," and enacted legislation to fight disease and poverty, renew urban areas, and support education and environmental conservation. Medicare and Medicaid were instituted under his administration. He continued Kennedy's support of space exploration, and he is also known, although less positively, for his handling of the **Vietnam War**.

Factors that Led to the Growth of the Civil Rights Movement

In the 1950s, post-war America was experiencing a rapid growth in prosperity; however, African Americans found themselves left behind. Racial segregation and discrimination were still legalized at this time and disproportionately affected black Americans and other minority groups. The civil rights movement arose to abolish legalized discrimination and provide equality for all Americans.

While there were many different ideologies that made up the civil rights movement, the movement is largely characterized by peaceful protest and civil disobedience.

- **Rosa Parks**—often called the "mother of the Civil Rights Movement," her refusal to give up her seat on the bus to a white man served as a seed from which the movement grew.
- **Martin Luther King, Jr.**—the best-known leader of the movement, King drew on Gandhi's beliefs and encouraged non-violent opposition. He led a march on Washington in 1963, received the Nobel Peace Prize in 1964, and was assassinated in 1968.
- **Malcolm X**—espousing less peaceful means of change, Malcolm X became a Black Muslim and supported black nationalism.

Policies and Legislation Enacted Expanding Minority Rights

Several major acts have been passed, particularly since WWII, to protect the rights of minorities in America. These include:

- Civil Rights Act (1964)
- Voting Rights Act (1965)
- Age Discrimination Act (1967)
- Americans with Disabilities Act (1990)

Other important movements for civil rights included a prisoner's rights movement, movements for immigrant rights, and the women's rights movement. The National Organization for Women (NOW) was established in 1966 and worked to pass the Equal Rights Amendment. The amendment was passed, but not enough states ratified it for it to become part of the US Constitution.

Impact of Stokely Carmichael, Adam Clayton Powell, and Jesse Jackson

- **Stokely Carmichael**—Carmichael originated the term "Black Power" and served as head of the Student Nonviolent Coordinating Committee. He believed in black pride and black culture and felt separate political and social institutions should be developed for blacks.
- **Adam Clayton Powell**—chairman of the Coordinating Committee for Employment, he led rent strikes and other actions, as well as a bus boycott, to increase the hiring of blacks.
- **Jesse Jackson**—Jackson was selected to head the Chicago Operation Breadbasket in 1966, and went on to organize boycotts and other actions. He also had an unsuccessful run for president.

Events of the Civil Rights Movement

Major events of the Civil Rights Movement include:

- **Montgomery Bus Boycott**—in 1955, Rosa Parks refused to give her seat on the bus to a white man. As a result, she was tried and convicted of disorderly conduct and of violating local ordinances. A 381-day bus boycott ensued, protesting segregation on public buses.
- **Desegregation of Little Rock**—in 1957, after the Supreme Court decision on Brown v. Board of Education, which declared "separate but equal" unconstitutional, the Arkansas school board voted to desegregate their schools. Even though Arkansas was considered progressive, its governor brought in the Arkansas National Guard to prevent nine black students from entering Central High School in Little Rock. President Eisenhower responded by federalizing the National Guard and ordering them to stand down.

- **Birmingham Campaign**—protestors organized a variety of actions such as sit-ins and an organized march to launch a voting campaign. When the City of Birmingham declared the protests illegal, the protestors, including Martin Luther King, Jr., persisted and were arrested and jailed.
- **March on Washington**—on August 28, 1963, more than 200,000 people marched on Washington, D.C. to advocate for civil and economic rights for African Americans. Dr. Martin Luther King Jr., positioned near the Lincoln Memorial, gave his famous "I Have a Dream" speech. This march was heavily influential in passing the Civil Rights Act of 1964.

Pieces of Legislation Passed as a Result of the Civil Rights Movement

Other pieces of legislation passed as a result of the Civil Rights movement include:

- **Brown v. Board of Education** (1954)—the Supreme Court declared that "separate but equal" accommodations and services were unconstitutional.
- **Civil Rights Act of 1964**—this declared discrimination illegal in employment, education, or public accommodation.
- **Voting Rights Act of 1965**—this act ended various activities practiced, mostly in the South, to bar blacks from exercising their voting rights. These included poll taxes and literacy tests.
- **Fair Housing Act of 1968**—this act prohibited discrimination in the sale, purchase, and rental of housing.

Other pieces of legislation that expanded minority rights include the Age Discrimination Act (1967) and the Americans with Disabilities Act (1990). Other important movements for civil rights included prisoners' rights movements, movements for immigrant rights, and the women's rights movement. The National Organization for Women (NOW) was established in 1966 and worked to pass the Equal Rights Amendment. The amendment was passed, but not enough states ratified it for it to become part of the US Constitution.

Events of the Richard Nixon Presidency

Richard Nixon is best known for the **Watergate scandal** during his presidency, but other important events marked his tenure as president, including:

- End of the Vietnam War
- Improved diplomatic relations between the US and China, and the US and the USSR
- National Environmental Policy Act passed, providing for environmental protection
- Compulsory draft ended
- Supreme Court legalized abortion in Roe v. Wade (subsequently overturned in 2022)
- Watergate

The Watergate scandal of 1972 ended Nixon's presidency. Rather than face impeachment and removal from office, he **resigned** in 1974.

US Perspective on the Progression of the Vietnam War

After World War II, the US pledged, as part of its foreign policy, to come to the assistance of any country threatened by **communism**. When Vietnam was divided into a communist North and democratic South, much like Korea before it, the eventual attempts by the North to unify the country under Communist rule led to intervention by the US. On the home front, the **Vietnam War** became more and more unpopular politically, with Americans growing increasingly discontent with the inability of the US to achieve the goals it had set for the Asian country. When President **Richard Nixon** took office in 1969, his escalation of the war led to protests at Kent State in Ohio, during which several students were killed by National Guard troops. Protests continued, eventually resulting in the end of the compulsory draft in 1973. In that same year, the US departed Vietnam. In 1975, the South surrendered, and Vietnam became a unified country under communist rule.

Events of the Gerald Ford Presidency

Gerald Ford was appointed to the vice presidency after Nixon's vice president **Spiro Agnew** resigned in 1973 under charges of tax evasion. With Nixon's resignation, Ford became president.

Ford's presidency saw negotiations with Russia to limit nuclear arms, as well as struggles to deal with inflation, economic downturn, and energy shortages. Ford's policies sought to reduce governmental control of various businesses and reduce the role of government overall. He also worked to prevent escalation of conflicts in the Middle East.

End of the Cold War and the Dissolution of the Soviet Union

In the late 1980s, **Mikhail Gorbachev** led the Soviet Union. He introduced a series of reform programs. **Ronald Reagan** famously urged Gorbachev to tear down the **Berlin Wall** as a gesture of growing freedom in the Eastern Bloc, and in 1989 it was demolished, ending the separation of East and West Germany. The Soviet Union relinquished its power over the various republics in Eastern Europe, and they became independent nations with their own individual governments. In 1991, the **USSR** was dissolved and the Cold War also came to an end.

Review Video: The End of the Cold War
Visit mometrix.com/academy and enter code: 278032

Events of the Jimmy Carter Presidency

Jimmy Carter was elected as president in 1976. Faced with a budget deficit, high unemployment, and continued inflation, Carter also dealt with numerous matters of international diplomacy, including:

- **Torrijos-Carter Treaties**—the US gave control of the Panama Canal to Panama.
- **Camp David Accords**—negotiations between Anwar el-Sadat, the president of Egypt, and Menachem Begin, the Israeli Prime Minister, led to a peace treaty between Egypt and Israel.
- **Strategic Arms Limitation Talks (SALT)**—these led to agreements and treaties between the US and the Soviet Union.
- **Iran Hostage Crisis**—after the Shah of Iran was deposed, an Islamic cleric, Ayatollah Khomeini, came to power. The shah came to the US for medical treatment, and Iran demanded his return so he could stand trial. In retaliation, a group of Iranian students stormed the US Embassy in Iran. Fifty-two American hostages were held for 444 days.

Jimmy Carter was awarded the **Nobel Peace Prize** in 2002.

Events of the Ronald Reagan Presidency

Ronald Reagan, at 69, became the oldest American president. The two terms of his administration included notable events such as:

- Reaganomics, also known as supply-side, trickle-down, or free-market economics, involving major tax cuts
- Economic Recovery Tax Act of 1981
- First female justice appointed to the Supreme Court—Sandra Day O'Connor
- Massive increase in the national debt—from $1 trillion to $3 trillion

- Reduction of nuclear weapons via negotiations with Mikhail Gorbachev
- Iran-Contra scandal—cover-up of US involvement in revolutions in El Salvador and Nicaragua
- Deregulation of savings and loan industry
- Loss of the space shuttle *Challenger*

Events of the George H. W. Bush Presidency

Reagan's presidency was followed by a term under his former vice president, **George H. W. Bush**. Bush's run for president included the famous "**thousand points of light**" speech, which was instrumental in increasing his standing in the election polls. During Bush's presidency, numerous international events took place, including:

- Fall of the Berlin wall and Germany's unification
- Panamanian dictator Manuel Noriega captured and tried on drug and racketeering charges
- Dissolution of the Soviet Union
- Gulf War, or Operation Desert Storm, triggered by Iraq's invasion of Kuwait
- Tiananmen Square Massacre in Beijing, China
- Ruby Ridge
- The arrival of the World Wide Web

Events of the William Clinton Presidency

William Jefferson "Bill" Clinton was the second president in US history to be impeached, but he was not convicted, and maintained high approval ratings in spite of the impeachment. Major events during his presidency included:

- Family and Medical Leave Act
- "Don't Ask, Don't Tell," a compromise position regarding homosexuals serving in the military
- North American Free Trade Agreement, or NAFTA
- Defense of Marriage Act
- Oslo Accords
- Siege at Waco, Texas, involving the Branch Davidians led by David Koresh
- Bombing of the Murrah Federal Building in Oklahoma City, Oklahoma
- Troops sent to Haiti, Bosnia, and Somalia to assist with domestic problems in those areas

Events of the George W. Bush Presidency

George W. Bush, son of George H. W. Bush, became president after Clinton. Major events during his presidency included:

- September 11, 2001, al-Qaeda terrorists hijack commercial airliners and fly into the World Trade Center towers and the Pentagon, killing nearly 3,000 Americans
- US troops sent to Afghanistan to hunt down al-Qaeda leaders, including the head of the organization, Osama Bin Laden; beginning of the War on Terror
- US troops sent to Iraq, along with a multinational coalition, to depose Saddam Hussein and prevent his deployment of suspected weapons of mass destruction
- Subprime mortgage crisis and near collapse of the financial industry, leading to the Great Recession; first of multiple government bailouts of the financial industry

Events of the Barack Obama Presidency

In 2008, Barack Obama, a senator from Illinois, became the first African American US president. His administration focused on improving the lot of a country suffering from a major recession. His major initiatives included:

- Economic bailout packages
- Improvements in women's rights
- Moves to broaden LGBT rights
- Health care reform legislation
- Reinforcement of the war in Afghanistan

Events of the Donald Trump Presidency

In 2016, Donald Trump, previously a real estate developer and television personality, was elected 45th president after a tumultuous election in which he won the electoral college but lost the popular vote. Marked by tension between the administration and domestic media, Trump's initiatives included:

- Appointing three Supreme Court Justices: Neil Gorsuch, Brett Kavanaugh, and Amy Coney Barrett
- Passing a major tax reform bill
- Enacting travel and emigration restrictions on eight nations: Iran, Libya, Syria, Yemen, Somalia, Chad, North Korea, and Venezuela
- Recognizing Jerusalem, rather than Tel Aviv, as the capital of Israel
- Responding to the novel coronavirus (SARS-CoV-2) outbreak

Almost completely along party lines, Donald Trump was impeached by the House on charges of abuse of power and obstruction of Congress; he was acquitted by the Senate.

Chapter Quiz

Ready to see how well you retained what you just read? Scan the QR code to go directly to the chapter quiz interface for this study guide. If you're using a computer, simply visit the online resources page at **mometrix.com/resources719/sslaushistory** and click the Chapter Quizzes link.

Practice Test #1

Want to take this practice test in an online interactive format?
Check out the online resources page, which includes interactive practice questions and much more: **mometrix.com/resources719/sslaushistory**

Use the excerpt and your knowledge of social studies to answer the following questions from the opening of the Declaration of Independence:

> "IN CONGRESS, July 4, 1776.
>
> The unanimous Declaration of the thirteen united States of America,
>
> When in the Course of human events, it becomes necessary for one people to dissolve the political bands which have connected them with another, and to assume among the powers of the earth, the separate and equal station to which the Laws of Nature and of Nature's God entitle them, a decent respect to the opinions of mankind requires that they should declare the causes which impel them to the separation."

1. Which of the following sentences BEST summarizes the meaning of the excerpt?

a. The thirteen colonies were planning to give separate but equal rights to African-American slaves.
b. The thirteen colonies had been attacked by British troops, and wanted to list their reasons for fighting back against England.
c. The thirteen colonies were forming their own government separate from the King of England, and they planned to outline the reasons for their revolution against England.
d. The thirteen colonies would form their own government separate from England, but they would list the laws of nature which kept them attached to England for some purposes.

2. What grassroots political movement, started by southern and western farmers, arose in the 1890s US to fight banks, railroads, large corporations and other "elites"?

a. Entrepreneurship Movement
b. Farmers United
c. Populist Movement
d. Social Gospel Movement

3. Which characteristic has NOT yet been used to define a historical era in US History?

a. A land form
b. Years of war
c. Years of social reforms
d. A time of economic growth or failure

4. Which momentous event related to the Spanish-America War occurred in 1898?

a. America gave financial support to Cuban nationalists' revolution against Spain.
b. Americans blamed Spain for the sinking of the *USS Maine*.
c. The Philippines declared independence from US rule after Spain had transferred their rule of the Philippines to the US
d. The US withdrew from Cuba.

5. The 1887 General Allotment Act, also known as the Dawes Act, had a policy of giving private property ownership to Native Americans in order to divide the Native American reservations into individual "family farms." What was a practical result of this policy?

a. Many Native American tribes lost large portions of their reservations.
b. Many Native Americans became assimilated to the American culture of family farming.
c. The Nez Perce Conflict occurred between Nez Perce Native Americans and US army forces.
d. American settlers moved to lands formerly owned by Native Americans and slaughtered most of the buffalo that Native Americans depended on for their livelihood.

6. In 1880, every state and territory in the US had railway tracks. Which statement BEST describes an effect of railroad growth on the US economy in the 1880s?

a. Railroad companies had to pay higher wages to employees
b. It provided better links between raw materials and markets
c. It increased competition between states and territories
d. It decreased taxes that railroad companies had to pay

Use the excerpt and your knowledge of social studies to answer the following question:

> US Navy Captain Alfred Thayer Mahan wrote an essay in 1890 including this statement:
>
> "The interesting and significant feature of this changing attitude [in America] is the turning of the eyes outward, instead of inward only, to seek the welfare of the country."

7. In the above quote, what was Mahan correctly predicting would occur more often in the 1890s?

a. US expansionism
b. US western settlement
c. US entry into World War I
d. US census bureau increasing counts

Use the timeline and your knowledge of social studies to answer the following question:

<u>Timeline of Events in Puerto Rico's History</u>

1902 United States declares Puerto Rico a territory

1904 Unionist Party of Puerto Rico forms as political opposition against the colonial US government

1914 Native Puerto Rican islanders' form a majority in the government's Executive Cabinet for this first time in the island's history as a US territory

1917 President Wilson signs the Jones Act which made Puerto Rico an "organized but unincorporated" territory, gave the island more autonomy in their government, and gave US citizen status to Puerto Ricans

8. Which conclusion is MOST true based on information in the above timeline?

a. Native Puerto Ricans had a majority in the island's government from the beginning of their time as a US territory
b. Spanish was declared the official language of Puerto Rico, even though the island became a US territory
c. Puerto Rico succumbed to US expansionism but also advocated to get more rights for the island natives
d. Puerto Rico natives formed a violent revolution against US colonialism

9. The first "May Day" celebration for the rights of working people occurred in the US on May 1, 1886, with more than 300,000 workers across the country participating in a one-day strike. Which factor below BEST describes one cause of this historic event?

a. Government policies on Native Americans meant that this group was assimilating into groups of workers, but they were also causing agitation among workers.
b. By 1886, union membership had grown to a high point, such as with a group called Knights of Labor having a membership of one million workers.
c. A law passed in 1885 raising an income tax on working people had caused a lot of anger among average workers.
d. Immigrants from European countries brought the May Day tradition from their countries to US workers.

10. Which of the following was one of the terms in the Treaty of Versailles at the end of World War I?

a. Germany had lands in Europe taken away but was able to keep their overseas colonies.
b. The German army was reduced but they were allowed to keep tanks.
c. Germany had to admit full responsibility for starting the war.
d. Germany was allowed to unite with Austria.

Use the excerpt and your knowledge of social studies to answer the following question:

From The Jungle, by Upton Sinclair, 1906

"The packers had secret mains, through which they stole billions of gallons of the city's water. The newspapers had been full of this scandal—once there had even been an investigation, and an actual uncovering of the pipes; but nobody had been punished, and the thing went right on. And then there was the condemned meat industry, with its endless horrors. The people of Chicago saw the government inspectors in Packingtown, and they all took that to mean that they were protected from diseased meat; they did not understand that these hundred and sixty-three inspectors had been appointed at the request of the packers, and that they were paid by the United States government to certify that all the diseased meat was kept in the state."

11. After President Theodore Roosevelt read "The Jungle," he ordered an investigation of the meat packing industry. What else MOST likely was a result of the book and the investigation?

a. Upton Sinclair ran a successful campaign to become the first Socialist congressional representative from New Jersey
b. Upton Sinclair published several other books that were just as commercially successful as "The Jungle" was
c. Theodore Roosevelt announced that he agreed with Upton Sinclair's political philosophy of socialism
d. Congress passed a "Pure Food and Drugs Act" and a "Meat Inspection Act" in 1906

Use the newspaper image and your knowledge of social studies to answer the following question:

THE AMERICAN ISSUE

U.S. IS VOTED DRY

36th STATE RATIFIES DRY AMENDMENT JAN. 16

Nebraska Noses Out Missouri for Honor of Completing Job of Writing Dry Act Into the Constitution; Wyoming, Wisconsin and Minnesota Right on Their Heels

JANUARY 16, 1919, MOMENTOUS DAY IN WORLD'S HISTORY

12. Which amendment is referenced in this newspaper headline?

a. 16th Amendment
b. 17th Amendment
c. 18th Amendment
d. 19th Amendment

13. Harry Laughlin, a scientist and eugenicist, testified in Congressional hearings on immigration policies in the early 1920s that immigrants from some European countries were biologically inferior to native-born white Americans. Laughlin claimed that immigrants had lower intelligence test scores and higher rates of criminal activity. What was one result of such eugenicist theories?

a. The Johnson Act was passed by Congress in 1924 to restrict annual immigration from certain regions of Europe
b. Congress passed an act in 1923 to increase the numbers of prisons in cities with high immigrant populations
c. The eugenics theories led believers in 1925 to form their own political party known as the Populists
d. Ellis Island closed in 1925 and no longer processed any immigrants into the US

14. In 1918, Marcus Garvey started a newspaper in the US called *The Negro World*, which promoted Garvey's philosophy of black pride, self-help, and economic independence for African Americans and Africans anywhere in the world. What other movement in the 1920s could be said to have been influenced by Marcus Garvey's ideas?

a. Accommodation
b. Black Panthers
c. Social Darwinism
d. Harlem Renaissance

Use the timeline and your knowledge of social studies to answer the following question:

<u>Aggressions by Dictators in 1930s to early 1940s</u>

1936 Italy (under Benito Mussolini) attacked and took over Ethiopia

1938 Germany (under dictator Adolf Hitler) took over Austria

1939 Hitler invaded Poland

15. Which event could be added to this timeline to show the final cause for Americans entering into World War II?

a. 1939 Japan entered an alliance with Germany and Italy
b. 1940 Germany invaded France
c. 1940 Germany invaded Denmark and Norway
d. 1941 Fascist government in Japan bombed Pearl Harbor

Use the excerpt and your knowledge of social studies to answer the following question:

> "Project TRINITY was the name given to the war-time effort [in the United States] to produce the first nuclear detonation. A plutonium-fueled implosion device was detonated on 16 July 1945 at the Alamogordo Bombing Range in south-central New Mexico."
>
> *-from <u>Project Trinity 1945-1946</u>, by Carl Maag and Steve Rohrer*

16. Why was Project Trinity a very important program for the US during World War II?

a. The US wanted to use nuclear energy to power their factories in helping the war effort.
b. Germany and Japan both had programs to build an atomic bomb, so the US needed one first to win the war.
c. Italy and Germany both had plans to build an atomic bomb, so the US needed to build one before their enemies did.
d. The US wanted to use the threat of a nuclear bomb to put down any insurrections that might start in Japanese internment camps in New Mexico.

Use the list and your knowledge of social studies to answer the following question:

Around 160,000 Allied troops landed along a 50-mile stretch of French coastline to fight Nazi Germany.

More than 5,000 ships and 13,000 aircraft gave support for the Allied attack.

17. Which World War II battle does the above information describe?

a. D-day, the Normandy Invasion
b. Battle of the Bulge
c. Battle of Midway
d. Battle of Britain

Use the photograph and your knowledge of social studies to answer the following question:

Some victory gardeners displaying their vegetables 1942 or 1943

18. What was one main purpose of a Victory Garden in the US during World War II?

a. To ensure that the domestic food supply was not being poisoned by foreign spies or infiltrators
b. To decrease demand on commercial vegetable growers, making more food available to soldiers
c. To provide more nutritious food for poor immigrant populations
d. To sell grown foods at markets and raise money for war bonds

Use the map and your knowledge of social studies to answer the following question:

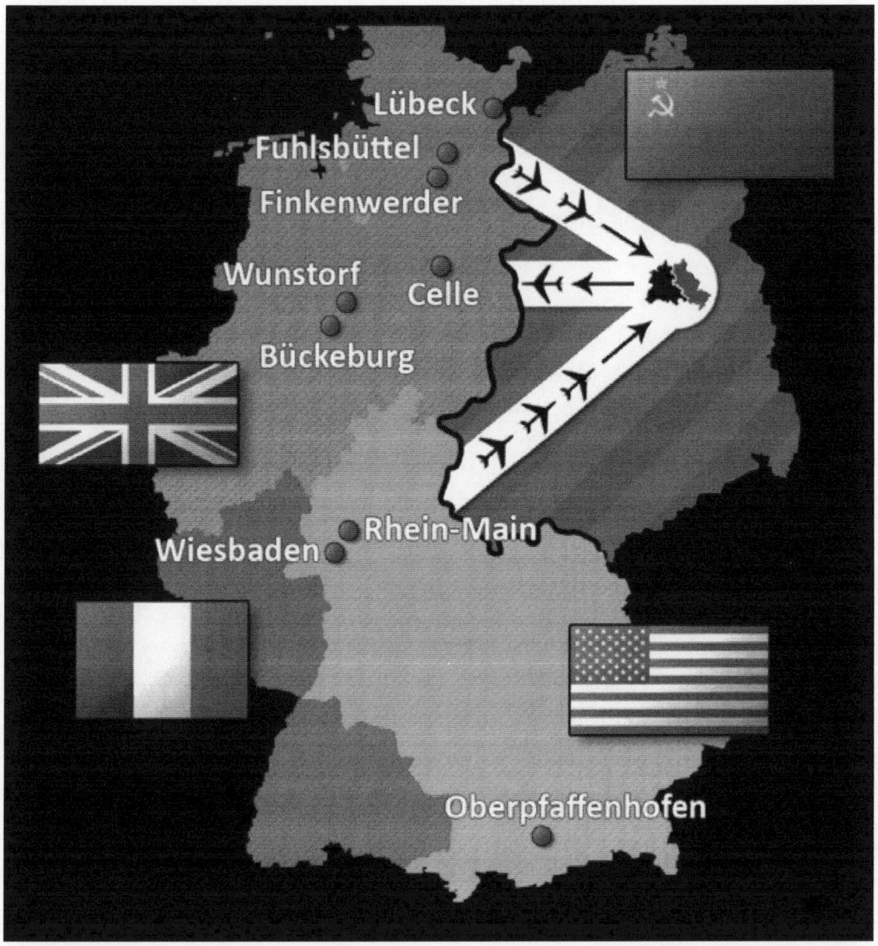

Post World War II Germany, around 1948-49, showing Germany divided into the American sector, British sector, French sector, and Russian sector. The capital city of Berlin was also divided into those four sectors after the war.

19. This map shows political divisions of Germany after World War II. What else does this map illustrate with the use of arrows?

a. The area designated as "free airspace" where travelers from the different sectors could travel in between East and West Germany
b. The "Berlin Bombing" routes used by Allied aircraft to bomb enemy targets in East Berlin that were under control of the U.S.S.R.
c. The "Berlin Airlift," the routes used by Allied aircraft to airlift supplies to West Berlin because the Soviet Union was imposing a blockade on supplies to West Berlin
d. The plans for moving Germany's defeated air force and airplanes in between new airports owned by Soviet, American, French, and British governments

Use the list and your knowledge of social studies to answer the following question:

- Communist North Korea invaded South Korea in 1950.
- President Truman worried that the Soviet Union and China planned to expand communism throughout Asia.
- The United Nations passed a resolution in 1950 urging United Nations member countries to give assistance to South Korea in their battle against North Korea.

20. What would be the BEST title for this list that summarizes what all of the items on the list have in common?

a. Reasons Why the Policy of Containment was Ineffective
b. Reasons for United States Involvement in the Korean War
c. Reasons for the Popularity of McCarthyism in the United States
d. Reasons Why the House Un-American Activities Committee Formed

21. In 1969, President Nixon made a speech about the Vietnam War and referred to a "silent majority" of Americans. Which Americans did he define as the "silent majority"?

a. Americans who were against the Vietnam War but were not actively protesting in the streets.
b. Americans who supported the Vietnam War but were not overly expressive about their opinions, unlike certain loud war protestors.
c. American troops who had returned from fighting in the Vietnam War in need of social services, even though they did not loudly demand such services.
d. American politicians who were quietly listening to opinions about the Vietnam War from their constituents before making any political decisions about the war.

Use the excerpt and your knowledge of social studies to answer the following question:

The Black Experience in America by Norman Coombs, 1972

"During Reconstruction blacks played a significant political role throughout the South. Besides voting in large numbers, they were elected to local, state, and federal offices. Between 1869 and 1901, two became U. S. Senators and twenty were members of the House of Representatives. Senators Revels and Bruce were elected from Mississippi. P. B. S. Pinchback was elected to the Senate from Louisiana, but he was not permitted to take his seat. He did serve as Lieutenant Governor of Louisiana, and, for three days, was Acting Governor."

22. Which amendment MOST made the above events possible?

a. 13th Amendment
b. 14th Amendment
c. 15th Amendment
d. 19th Amendment

Use the chart and your knowledge of social studies to answer the following question:

Chart—Percentage of African Americans in Certain Military Ranks, 1964-1966

Rank E-6 (Staff Sergeant or Petty Officer, First Class)

	1964	**1965**	**1966**
Army	13.9	15.5	18.1
Navy	4.7	5.0	5.6
Marine Corps	5.0	5.3	10.4

Source: Office, Deputy Assistant Secretary of Defense (Civil Rights)

23. In the early 1960s, President Kennedy became more committed to helping civil rights causes, including the cause of desegregation in the military. Based on this chart, what conclusion about African Americans in 1964-66 military ranks can be made?

a. African Americans started making up a larger percentage of Major or Lieutenant Commander Ranks in the Army, Navy, and Marines
b. African Americans started making up a larger percentage of Staff Sergeant or Petty Officer Ranks in the Army, Navy, and Marines
c. African Americans started making up a larger percentage of Staff Sergeant or Petty Officer Ranks in the Army and Marines, but not in the Navy.
d. The percentage of African-American Staff Sergeants or Petty Officers grew between 1954 and 1965, but then declined again between 1965 and 1966

24. Which part of the Iran-Contra affair (that took place under President Reagan in the 1980s) consisted of illegal activities?

a. The US convinced other countries to sell weapons to Iran. The Contras inside the Nicaraguan government also sold weapons to Iran.
b. Iran was allowed to begin research into nuclear weapons. Contras fighting the government in Nicaragua were allowed to buy weapons from Iran.
c. Weapons were illegally sold to Iran by the US government. Funds from the arms sales were illegally diverted to support the Contras, a group fighting the Nicaraguan government.
d. The US sold weapons to the Contras, a group supporting the Nicaraguan government. Funds from the arms sales were illegally diverted to a group inside Iran fighting that government.

Use the excerpt and your knowledge of social studies to answer the following question:

> "America is at war with a transnational terrorist movement fueled by a radical ideology of hatred, oppression, and murder. Our National Strategy for Combating Terrorism, first published in February 2003, recognizes that we are at war and that protecting and defending the Homeland, the American people, and their livelihoods remains our first and most solemn obligation."

From *National Strategy for Combating Terrorism*, Sept. 2006

25. What was another name for the "National Strategy for Combating Terrorism"?

a. Homeland Radicalism
b. Persian Gulf War
c. Terrorism Crisis
d. War on Terror

Use the excerpt and your knowledge of social studies to answer the following question:

> "There is a time to every purpose under the heaven--a time of war and a time of peace." So spoke one of Woodstock's most famous sons, the Reverend John Peter Gabriel Muhlenberg, in the Lutheran Church one Sunday morning after the Declaration of Independence had been issued. After delivering an inspired sermon taken from this text in which he reviewed his stand on liberty, he dramatically cast off his black pulpit robes and revealed to his astonished congregation his colonel's uniform of the Revolutionary army."

26. The excerpt describes two careers that John Peter Muhlenberg had before and during the Revolutionary War period. What were those two careers, and what third career did he have after the Revolutionary War?

a. Reverend, British Army Colonel, first Governor of Virginia
b. Speaker, British Army soldier, first Governor of Connecticut
c. Reverend, Continental Army Colonel, member of the first US Congress
d. Writer, signer of the Declaration of Independence, Continental Army soldier

27. What was the primary purpose of the Chinese Exclusion Act passed by the US Congress in 1882?

a. To ban Chinese from immigrating to the US
b. To exclude Chinese Americans from joining unions in the US
c. To ban Chinese Americans from working on railroads in the US
d. To exclude Chinese from claiming settlement lands in the western US

Use the photo and your knowledge of social studies to answer the following question:

Alvan Macauley (left), President of the Packard Motor Car Co. and Col. Charles A. Lindbergh with the original Packard diesel-powered Stinson "Detroiter" in the background, 1929. (Smithsonian photo A48319D.)

28. Besides flying some of the original diesel-powered airplanes, what was another notable contribution of Colonel Charles A. Lindbergh to 1920s US history?

a. He made the first solo nonstop flight across the Atlantic Ocean in 1927.
b. He made the first solo nonstop flight across the Pacific Ocean in 1928.
c. He trained Amelia Earhart, the first female solo pilot, in piloting skills.
d. After Lindbergh's son was kidnapped, Congress passed the "Lindbergh Law," which made kidnapping a federal offense if a child was taken across state lines.

Use the chart and your knowledge of social studies to answer the following question:

The only unbroken code in modern military history used Native-American words for military words, but words were not direct translations. The Native-American words were for something similar to the military term being described, for example:

Native American word:	Translation:	Code for:
chay-da-gahi	Tortoise	Tank
gini	Chicken hawk (a bird that dives on its prey).	Dive bomber
ne-he-mah	Our mother	America

29. What was the name of the US Marines group that used this code, and in which war was it used to communicate securely and save lives?

a. Navajo Code Talkers, World War I
b. Navajo Code Talkers, World War II
c. Sioux Secret Coders, World War I
d. Sioux Secret Coders, World War II

30. Although pressured to take military action by some advisors, President John F. Kennedy prevailed in his 1962 strategy of getting the Soviet Union to end the construction of bases for nuclear missiles on an island in return for a US promise to not invade that island. Those "13 Days in October" are more famously known by what name?

a. Dominican Republic Nuclear Danger
b. Dominican Republic at the Brink
c. Cuban Communist Crisis
d. Cuban Missile Crisis

Use the excerpt and your knowledge of social studies to answer the following question:

> "The animals which are found west of the Missouri River, especially in the Rocky Mountains, and far beyond them, are the buffalo, elk, deer, cimarron bear, mountain sheep, antelope, coyote, prairie-dog, etc.
>
> The buffalo, which affords good beef to the Indian hunters, and has fed many thousand toilers over the plains to Salt Lake and California, is mainly known to boys in the comfortable buffalo robes, which everyone knows the use of in sleigh-riding. But to us officers and soldiers on the plains they are life-preservers almost, in our sleeping out nights on the ground, far away from home and good beds and blankets."
>
> From *Three Years on the Plains* by Edmund B. Tuttle, 1870

31. Based on this excerpt, which statement would be MOST likely true about whites' settlement of the Great Plains in the late 1800s?

a. Like the Native Americans of the Great Plains, white settlers also came to rely on buffalo for food and for providing warm robes on cold nights
b. In the Great Plains there were many animals that could provide food for new white settlers, but there were not any dangerous animals
c. The white settlers came to rely on buffalo for providing food and on elk and deer for use in sleigh-riding
d. The white settlers in the Great Plains came to rely on buffalo for food, but not for any other purpose

Use the map and your knowledge of social studies to answer the following question:

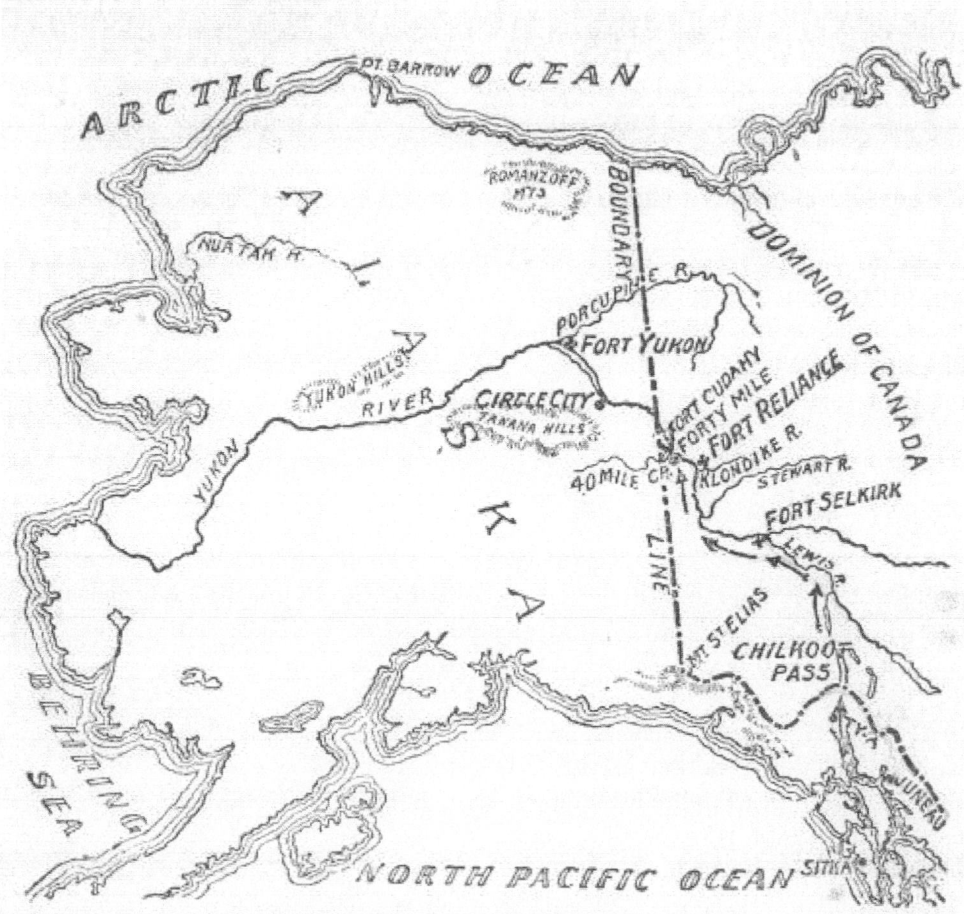

MAP OF THE YUKON GOLD DIGGINGS

32. In the 1890s, gold was discovered in the Klondike area of Alaska, and a rush of settlers came to the area. Based on the map, which of the following is MOST likely the correct order and route of how miners traveled in the area?

a. Miners buy supplies in Juneau, pack their loads and hike through Chilkoot Pass, take boats down Lewis River to the Klondike River, hike from the river to the Yukon Hills
b. Miners buy supplies in Juneau, ride on steamboats to Ty-a, pack their loads and hike through Chilkoot Pass, take boats down Lewis River to the Klondike River
c. Miners hike through the Chilkoot Pass, take boats down Lewis River to the Klondike River, buy supplies at the town of Forty Mile, pack their loads and hike forty miles into Canada
d. Miners hike through the Chilkoot Pass, take boats down Lewis River to the Klondike River, walk along that river bank to Circle City, buy supplies at Circle City

Use the excerpt and your knowledge of social studies to answer the following question:

> "At Panama earthquakes are few and unimportant, while the Nicaraguan route passes over a well-known coastal weakness. Only five disturbances of any sort were recorded at Panama, all very slight, while similar official records at San Jose de Costa Rica, near the route of the Nicaragua Canal, show for the same period fifty shocks, a number of which were severe."

> And later he continued: "The situation being, then, that the danger from volcanoes at Panama is nothing, and that from earthquakes practically nothing, while at Nicaragua the canal would be situated in one of the most dangerous regions of the world from both these causes, the question should be considered settled."

33. Based on this excerpt, which statement would be MOST likely true about the Panama Canal?

a. When considering where to build a canal in Central America, factors such as earthquakes and volcanoes needed to be taken into consideration.
b. It was risky to build a canal in Panama because of possible volcanoes there, but the risk of earthquakes in Nicaragua was greater.
c. There were never any volcanoes or earthquakes in Nicaragua, so there was no danger to building a canal there.
d. There were never any volcanoes or earthquakes in Panama, so there was no danger to building a canal there.

Use the excerpt and your knowledge of social studies to answer the following question:

> "Some say that they left the South on account of injustice in the courts, unrest, lack of privileges, denial of the right to vote, bad treatment, oppression, segregation or lynching. Others say that they left to find employment, to secure better wages, better school facilities, and better opportunities to toil upward."

34. What would be the BEST summary of this excerpt?

a. Causes of Confederate Soldiers Abandoning the South
b. Effects of Migration from the Rust Belt to the Sun Belt
c. Causes of the Great Migration
d. Effects of Western Expansion

35. A study in 1998 found that new immigrants to the US tended to settle in the "port-of-entry" states where they first entered the United States. How would this fact MOST likely affect demographics within the US?

a. There would be a high number of immigrants settling in states such as California, New York, and Texas
b. There would be a high number of immigrants settling in states such as Colorado, Utah, and Nebraska
c. Native-born Americans would leave the states where new immigrants were settling
d. It would have no effect on demographics within the United States

36. Tin Pan Alley referred to the location in New York City of popular music publishers, and also to the kind of music being produced there in the 1890s and early 20th century. What were one negative impact and one positive impact of Tin Pan Alley?

a. *Positive*: Tin Pan Alley was the birthplace of American popular music and created the ASCAP (American Society of Composers, Authors, and Publishers).
Negative: ASCAP was a predominantly white group for many years until the popularity of music by African Americans arose in the late 1920s.
b. *Positive*: Tin Pan Alley sold millions of copies of sheet music.
Negative: The Tin Pan Alley location still has many music publishers but has become a high-crime area.
c. *Positive*: Tin Pan Alley gave a lot of jobs to new immigrants.
Negative: All the money earned went to publishing companies, while composers stayed poor.
d. *Positive*: Sheet music could now be sold to the public, instead of just to professional performers.
Negative: Tin Pan Alley did not hire any immigrants.

Use the list and your knowledge of social studies to answer the following question:

Disneyland

Hollywood movies

McDonald's restaurants

Pop music

Television shows

37. Which heading would BEST describe something that the items on this list have in common?

a. Things That Began in the 1920s
b. Things That Began in the 1930s
c. Things That Are Headquartered in California
d. American Pop Culture Influences on the World

Use the illustration and your knowledge of social studies to answer the following question:

Group of Converted Indians with their Pastor

38. This illustration BEST gives an example of which historical process?

a. Migration of Native Americans to Reservations
b. Movement to Assimilate Native Americans into American Culture
c. Native American Battles with White Settlers
d. Evangelicals Within the Native American Community

Use the excerpt and your knowledge of social studies to answer the following question:

A famous woman social worker wrote this in her book about her work in 1910:

"In spite of these flourishing clubs for children early established at Hull-House, and the fact that our first organized undertaking was a kindergarten, we were very insistent that the Settlement should not be primarily for the children, and that it was absurd to suppose that grown people would not respond to opportunities for education and social life."

39. Which famous woman did social work at Hull House in Chicago in the early 1900s and wrote that excerpt?

a. Susan B. Anthony
b. Jane Addams
c. Dr. Aletta Jacobs
d. Frances Willard

40. Which woman won an Outstanding Labor Leader Award for her lifetime work with Cesar Chavez on behalf of migrant farm workers in the US?

a. Isabelle Allende
b. Gloria Anzaldua
c. Dolores Huerta
d. Sonia Sotomayor

41. The Great Seal of the United States that was first used in 1782 included the motto *E Pluribus Unum*. The same motto appeared on federal coins in 1795. What is the meaning of this motto?

a. In God We Trust
b. In Union We Trust
c. Out of Many, One
d. The Many are United

42. In 1997, President Clinton presented the Congressional Medal of Honor to Vernon J. Baker, a 78-year-old African American, for his courage and leadership in attacks on the enemy in Italy during a previous war. Racial prejudice during the time of this war had prevented Baker from receiving the award previously. In which war did Vernon Baker bravely fight?

a. World War I
b. World War II
c. Korean War
d. Vietnam War

43. President Franklin Roosevelt's New Deal legislation included retirement income for elderly, farm subsidies, insurance for bank deposits, public works projects, benefits for the unemployed, and more. What kind of historic change did such programs represent?

a. It was the first time that federal legislation affected farmers
b. It was the first time that the Supreme Court had the final authority to approve legislation
c. The programs gave state and federal governments increased power to affect the economy
d. The programs gave more power to state governments but took away power from the federal government.

44. The Ethics in Government Act of 1978 required elected public officials to make public some of their financial information. What could be considered a source of public demand for increased ethics in government at that time period?

a. The Watergate Scandal of the early 1970s had eroded some public trust in government officials.
b. The Teapot Dome Scandal of the late 1960s had eroded some public trust in government officials.
c. Newspapers had been making up stories in the early 1970s about public officials misusing government money.
d. Gerald Ford was not considered an ethical president, which was also the main reason he did not get re-elected to a second term.

45. Providing increased border patrols at the US-Canada border was a provision of which legislation?

a. USA PATRIOT Act of 2001
b. Trade Act of 2002
c. Protection of Lawful Commerce in Arms Act of 2005
d. Secure Fence Act of 2006

46. Which statement below could be considered an advantage of the United States participating in the United Nations organization?

a. The United Nations does not involve itself in deadly conflicts or civil wars.
b. The United Nations has different foreign policy objectives than the United States has.
c. The United Nations has been a leader in helping to end the humanitarian and military crisis in Darfur.
d. The United Nations does not deal with relief for victims of natural disasters, thereby saving money for the United States.

47. In *Bush v. Gore*, the Supreme Court ruled 5-4 that a recount in that year's presidential election must take place by midnight of December 12th, 2000. The ruling came hours before the deadline, making it too late for a recount to actually occur. What is the BEST way to describe the historical aspect of this Supreme Court case?

a. This case caused states to make drastic changes in the ways that they supervised recounts in federal elections.
b. This case made history as the first time that a US President had his name and cause appear in a Supreme Court case.
c. This case showed for the first time that presidential candidates needed to hire lawyers even before their campaigns started.
d. This case marked the first time that the judicial branch of government involved itself in a federal election, and critics said that the Supreme Court rather than the electorate had determined the winner of a presidential election.

48. In 1954, the Supreme Court's *Brown v. Board of Education* decision declared that school segregation and the "separate but equal" doctrine was unconstitutional. What happened afterward in southern states that same year?

a. Southern states immediately started planning how to desegregate their schools.
b. The Cold War started and everyone ignored the school desegregation movement for a few years.
c. The President immediately got involved in helping to desegregate schools in southern states, and he called in National Guard troops to assist.
d. Southern opponents of segregation used intimidation and violence against desegregation proponents, and many southern school districts avoided compliance with the new law.

49. In 1973's *White v. Regester* Supreme Court case, the court ruled that Texas county, city council, and school board districts should have elections so that members would be voted in from individual electoral districts. What kind of system did Texas have before this Supreme Court decision?

a. A vote by mail system that was full of fraud problems.
b. A voting system that allowed too many "write-in" candidates.
c. A poll tax that discouraged voters from poor districts from voting.
d. An "at large" voting system that had weakened minority voting power.

Use the excerpt and your knowledge of social studies to answer the following question:

> "Mr. Rockefeller wished me to join his board and this I did. Cooperation was soon found to be much to our mutual advantage, and we now work in unison."

50. Along with John D. Rockefeller, the industrialist who wrote the above quote in his autobiography was also one of the founders of corporate philanthropy in the 20th century. He donated to libraries, schools, universities, and former employees. Who was this wealthy industrialist?

a. Henry Ward Beecher
b. Andrew Carnegie
c. Elbert H. Gary
d. John Stuart Mill

51. During World War II, Japanese Americans in internment camps were denied the right to be brought before a court to challenge the legality of their imprisonment. This was a violation of which constitutional right?

a. Right against involuntary servitude
b. Right to habeas corpus
c. Right to assemble
d. Right to vote

52. Which of the following methods was NOT used by suffragettes in their attempt to get the 19th Amendment (allowing women the right to vote) passed?

a. Marches
b. Nonviolent protests
c. Speeches and written articles
d. Payments to key senators to help the cause

53. The "laissez-faire" economists of the late 1800s, before Progressives had more influence, believed that businesses were best regulated by which entity?

a. Federal government
b. State or local governments
c. Trust-busting laws
d. Marketplace forces

Use the list and your knowledge of social studies to answer the following question:

- Provided that shipping rates should be fair and reasonable
- Required that rate information be made public
- Outlawed secret rebates
- Made price discrimination against small markets illegal
- Promised investigation of any rate abuses

54. The above list shows provisions of which piece of legislation?

a. Pacific Railway Act of 1862
b. Interstate Commerce Act of 1887
c. Dollar Diplomacy Act of 1911
d. Federal Reserve Act of 1913

55. When President Warren Harding called for a "Return to Normalcy" in 1920, the BEST summary of what he meant would be...

a. A return to the high employment rate that had dominated the US during World War I
b. A return to peaceful times and a focus on domestic issues, as opposed to a focus on international war
c. A return to a period of high immigration rates that were contributing to a diverse culture and growing economy in the US
d. A return to finding more territories, such as Puerto Rico and Guam acquired during the Spanish-American War, for expanding US markets

Use the excerpt and your knowledge of social studies to answer the following question:

From President Herbert Hoover's State of the Union Address, December 1931

"Our people have a right to a banking system in which their deposits shall be safeguarded and the flow of credit less subject to storms. The need of a sounder system is plainly shown by the extent of bank failures. I recommend the prompt improvement of the banking laws. Changed financial conditions and commercial practices must be met. "

56. Why did President Herbert Hoover feel the need to address bank failures during his 1930 State of the Union address?

a. Bank failures were one of the causes of the Great Depression.
b. Bank failures were one of the effects of the Great Depression.
c. Hoover planned a Federal Deposit Insurance Program to insure banks against future failures.
d. The 1930 Congress planned a Federal Deposit Insurance Program to insure banks against future failures.

57. President Franklin D. Roosevelt said his New Deal programs would use the authority of the federal government to help all classes and groups of people in the country. Who was one opponent of the New Deal programs, and why?

a. *The American public*: they felt the programs were not helping enough, and a majority planned to not re-elect President Roosevelt.
b. *Herbert Hoover*: he felt the federal government should not assume so much responsibility or deficit spending.
c. *1933 Congress*: they did not pass the New Deal programs proposed by the President.
d. *1935 Congress*: they did not pass the "Second Hundred Days" New Deal programs proposed by the President.

Use the chart and your knowledge of social studies to answer the following question:

New Deal Program	How it Worked	How it Still Affects People Today
Social Security Act of 1935	Provided pensions to elderly; benefit payments to dependent mothers, disabled children, and blind people; gave unemployment insurance.	Social Security Administration still gives benefit payments to retirees who have paid taxes during their working years. There are still programs to benefit disabled and unemployed people, too.
Federal Deposit Insurance Corporation		The FDIC is still active today to maintain banking stability and public confidence by insuring deposits, protecting consumers, and overseeing bank safety and soundness.

58. Which statement would BEST fill in the blank space on the chart, explaining how the FDIC originally worked in the 1930s?

a. Gave gold to failing banks
b. Encouraged worried Americans to withdraw their money from failing banks
c. Gave insurance on checking accounts that were not earning enough interest for customers
d. Provided deposit insurance to banks and had the authority to regulate and supervise banks

59. During World War II, unemployment in the US for civilians went from 14 percent in 1940 to 1.2 percent in 1944. Which choice below BEST describes a cause and an effect of this drop in unemployment?

a. *Cause*: The internment of Japanese Americans made for less competition for factory jobs.
Effect: Decreased the need for rationing food because more was being produced in factories.
b. *Cause*: The New Deal programs were finally helping end unemployment.
Effect: A third round of New Deal programs were passed by Congress.
c. *Cause*: Wartime economic boom expanded industrial production, with less workforce competition due to need for wartime soldiers.
Effect: Helped end the Great Depression.
d. *Cause*: Increased opportunity for women and minorities to gain employment.
Effect: There was increased racism as there was increased competition for remaining jobs.

60. In the early 1950s, the birthrate in the US kept climbing steadily each year, from around 3.6 million births in 1950 to 4.3 million births in 1957. Which phrase BEST describes this post war phenomenon, and tells an effect of the phenomenon?

a. "Baby Boom," benefitted the US economy and led to a greater demand for consumer products
b. "Women Quitting Work Effect," caused an increase in employment opportunities for men
c. "Soldiers Returning Effect," caused more out-of-wedlock births
d. "Baby Bust," led to decreased prosperity in the 1950s

Use the list and your knowledge of social studies to answer the following question:

- A Wilderness Protection Act saved forestland from being developed
- The Elementary and Secondary Education Act provided money for public schools
- Medicare was started to help elderly with the costs of health care
- A Housing Act provided money to build low-income housing
- Pollution controls became stronger due to the Air and Water Quality Acts
- Standards were raised for safety in consumer products
- A Food Stamp program was enacted
- Head Start's preschool programs for poor children were created
- The Corporation for Public Broadcasting was created, providing many public television and radio stations

61. All of the programs on the above list fall under what category of programs?

a. President Franklin D. Roosevelt's New Deal programs
b. President John F. Kennedy's Civil Rights programs
c. President Lyndon B. Johnson's Great Society programs
d. President Richard M. Nixon's American Welfare programs

62. When the Organization of Petroleum Exporting Countries (OPEC) declared an oil embargo against the United States from 1973 to 1974, what was an effect on the US free enterprise system?

a. Car owners stocked up on gasoline.
b. Auto manufacturers in the US started selling cars to European customers instead of to US customers.
c. The effect on the US free enterprise system was minor; the US had stockpiles of oil reserves and was actively drilling for oil in Texas and Alaska.
d. The US experienced inflation, economic recession, and restrictions on gasoline purchases; auto manufacturers started making smaller and more fuel-efficient cars.

63. In 1997, he was called the "richest man in America" for his approximate net worth of $37 billion, which he earned in the computer industry. He tries to keep the American Dream alive for others by philanthropically donating money to schools, libraries, and computer labs. Who is this American entrepreneur?

a. Warren Buffett
b. Bill Gates
c. Robert Johnson
d. Sam Walton

Use the excerpt and your knowledge of social studies to answer the following question:

> "The foreman of a Pittsburg coal company may now stand in his subterranean office and talk to the president of the Steel Trust, who sits on the twenty-first floor of a New York skyscraper. The long-distance talks, especially, have grown to be indispensable to the corporations whose plants are scattered and geographically misplaced—to the mills of New England, for instance, that use the cotton of the South and sell so much of their product to the Middle West. To the companies that sell perishable commodities, an instantaneous conversation with a buyer in a distant city has often saved a carload or a cargo."

64. The author of this excerpt is describing the social and economic/business effects of which technological innovation?

a. Coal smelting
b. Stock ticker
c. Telegraph
d. Telephone

Use the timeline and your knowledge of social studies to answer the following question:

- 1921 - Franklin Roosevelt acquired the disease called polio and lost the use of his legs at age 39
- 1930s - Polio outbreaks became more frequent in the US and public sympathy was high to help the victims
- 1938 - President Franklin Roosevelt founded the National Foundation for Infantile Paralysis (NFIP), later renamed the March of Dimes Foundation, to help fund research for a polio vaccine
- 1955 - Dr. Jonas Salk developed and tested the first successful polio vaccine

65. What is one conclusion that can be made based on this timeline?

a. Historical events and the specific needs of society can contribute to medical inventions.
b. Polio outbreaks were worse in the US than in other countries in the 1920s.
c. A disease outbreak can only be prevented by the development of a vaccine.
d. Franklin Roosevelt developed the first successful polio vaccine.

Use the excerpt and your knowledge of social studies to answer the following question:

In "My Life and Work," 1922, Henry Ford wrote:

"The first step forward in assembly came when we began taking the work to the men instead of the men to the work. We now have two general principles in all operations—that a man shall never have to take more than one step, if possibly it can be avoided, and that no man need ever stoop over.

The principles of assembly are these:

(1) Place the tools and the men in the sequence of the operation so that each component part shall travel the least possible distance while in the process of finishing.

(2) Use work slides or some other form of carrier so that when a workman completes his operation, he drops the part always in the same place—which place must always be the most convenient place to his hand—and if possible have gravity carry the part to the next workman for his operation.

(3) Use sliding assembling lines by which the parts to be assembled are delivered at convenient distances."

66. What is the BEST inference that can be made based on this excerpt?

a. Henry Ford worked on assembly lines alongside his workmen.
b. The development of time-study analysis in factories led to increased inventory management.
c. The development of the assembly line method in factories led to increased worker productivity.
d. Henry Ford was mostly concerned with ergonomics in the workplace so that working men would not get hurt.

Use the timeline and your knowledge of social studies to answer the following question:

- 1978: A Teflon-coated fiberglass used in astronaut spacesuits was re-used as a roofing material for buildings and stadiums in the US
- 1982: Astronauts working on the lunar surface wore liquid-cooled garments under their space suits to protect them from very hot temperatures. The garments became adapted as portable cooling systems for treatment of medical conditions like burning limbs, multiple sclerosis, and spinal injuries.
- 1995: Dr. Michael DeBakey teamed up with Johnson Space Center Engineer David Saucier to develop an artificial heart pump based on space shuttle engine fuel pumps. The heart pump they developed can supplement the left ventricle's pumping capacity in a heart.

67. What is the BEST summary of the facts presented in this timeline?

a. Technology used in space explorations can also improve the quality of life on Earth
b. Architects should study all the technologies used by engineers in space explorations
c. Doctors should study all the technologies used by engineers for space explorations
d. Space explorations are too expensive, but they do have some positive benefits also

68. The US-Canada Free-Trade Agreement (FTA) of 1989 was replaced in 1994 by what?

a. North American Free Trade Agreement (NAFTA)
b. Open Trade with Canada Agreement (OTC)
c. US - Canada Limited Trade Agreement (LTA)
d. US-Mexico Free-Trade Agreement (UMFTA)

Answer Key and Explanations for Test #1

1. C: It best summarizes the excerpt and shows knowledge of what else is outlined in the Declaration of Independence (grievances against England and reasons for declaring independence). Choice B would be a good guess, but the Declaration was written not because of attacks by British troops, but more because of rebellions by colonists. A student may pick choice A if they focus on the "separate but equal" clause in the excerpt, but the provision of "separate but equal" policies for African-American slaves came much later in US history. A student might pick choice D if focused on the "Laws of Nature" phrase in the excerpt, but the colonists did not list such laws still connecting them to England in the Declaration.

2. C: The Populist movement arose in the US in the 1890s as a grassroots political movement started by southern and western farmers to fight banks, railroads, large corporations and other "elites." "Farmers United" sounds like it could be a correct choice, given the involvement of farmers, but it is incorrect. Choice A and D are also incorrect, although the "Social Gospel" movement was active around the same time period. Entrepreneurship was also on the rise during that time period.

3. A: There has not yet been an era in US History defined by a land form (for example, something like a "Rocky Mountain Era"). There was a Gold Rush era but that was not named specifically for a land form. So A is the BEST choice. There have been eras defined by wars (Civil War Era), economic growth or failure (Roaring Twenties, Great Depression), and by social reforms (Progressive Era).

4. B: The sinking of the USS Maine happened in 1898, and the fact that America blamed Spain was a major cause of the US and Spain declaring war on each other in 1898. All the other events listed did not happen in 1898, so even though they are related to the Spanish-American War, they would not be the correct answer. Choice A happened in 1895, choice C occurred in 1899, and choice D happened in 1902.

5. A: Choice D sounds like a good option, because this is something that did happen, but it happened before the Dawes Act. The Nez Perce conflict of 1877 also occurred before the Dawes Act, so choice C is incorrect. Choice B was the hope of Dawes and other American politicians who planned the act in order to try to help "assimilate" Native Americans, but that was not the practical result as much as choice A, the taking over of reservation lands away from Native Americans.

6. B: Railroads did not have to pay higher wages to employees until after employees started unionizing in later years. For example, in the 1880s, they were still paying low wages to Chinese railway laborers. Choice B is the best answer: raw materials and markets were better connected for the distribution of economic products. Railroad companies probably did not see a big decrease in paying taxes, and probably had to pay more taxes to the various local governments where their tracks now ran through. States and territories became better connected by railroads, so "increased competition" would not be the best answer, either.

7. A: Mahan was correctly predicting that US expansionism would increase in the 1890s as Americans increasingly turned their interests "outward," and not just inward to their own country. The country's entry into WWI would not come until the early 1900s, so that answer is incorrect. Western expansion mostly occurred before the 1890s and would still be looking "inward" at their own country, even though looking to expand settlements. Census bureau counts did increase in the 1890s, but that again is concerned with the US looking "inward," examining their own population, rather than looking outward to expand into other countries.

8. C: The timeline facts show that Puerto Rico did succumb to US expansionism by becoming a territory, but also that native islanders fought for more political rights. There was no major violent revolution against the US in those years, and no minor ones are mentioned in the timeline, so that conclusion cannot be made. Spanish was not made the official language; English and Spanish were "co-official" for a time, and then English was made official in 1917. Also, languages are not mentioned in the timeline facts. Native Puerto Ricans did not have a majority in the island's government from the beginning of their time as a US territory; that did not occur until 1914 (according to the timeline facts).

9. B: It is the only answer that relates to the growth of union membership in the late 1800s, and how this had a causal relationship to the first US May Day celebration in 1886 of a massive one day strike. The other statements are all false. Choice D might be a good guess due to immigration at the time, but it is not thc BEST choice listed for a cause of May Day

10. C: According to the Treaty of Versailles, Germany had to admit full responsibility for the war. Germany was forbidden to unite with Austria in the Treaty. The country also had lands in both Europe AND colonial lands taken away. They had to reduce their army number of soldiers and were not allowed to keep tanks anymore. So the other choices are all incorrect.

11. D: Congress did pass a Pure Food and Drugs Act and a Meat Inspection Act in 1906 after the president ordered an investigation of the meat packing industry due to being concerned with passages from "The Jungle" by Upton Sinclair (like the passage excerpt quoted). Sinclair did subsequently write other books, but they were not as commercially successful as "The Jungle," and nothing in the excerpt or question stem could support that statement, so it is not a good answer choice. Sinclair did run a campaign to become the first congressional representative from New Jersey to be a member of the Socialist Party, but he did not win. Roosevelt did not agree with Sinclair's socialist politics. Those answers should be eliminated by the student based on their general knowledge of social studies and that time period.

12. C: While the 16th, 17th, and 19th Amendments were in a similar time period as the 18th Amendment, the specific year 1919 and the reference to "being voted dry" are clues to a student who has some historical knowledge that this headline refers to the 18th Amendment. The 18th Amendment is the one prohibiting alcohol, thus the reference to becoming "dry."

13. A: It shows an effect caused by eugenics theories, which was a law restricting immigrants in 1924. But Ellis Island did not close completely until 1954 (later becoming a historic site and national park). The Populist political party was formed in the 1890s, so that answer is incorrect. Choice B sounds like it could be a result of eugenics theories but it is actually a made-up fact.

14. D: The 1920s Harlem Renaissance has been said by history professors to have been influenced by Marcus Garvey's movement of promoting black pride and black self-reliance. The Black Panthers were probably influenced by Garvey's ideas, but their movement did not begin until later in US history. Accommodation was a movement promoted by leaders such as Booker T. Washington, around the same time as Garvey, but with somewhat opposite ideals from Garvey's promotion of economic independence. (Accommodation would be to interact economically with whites but accommodate to their separate but equal segregation rules.) Social Darwinism was a movement in the 1920s that could not be said to be influenced by Marcus Garvey, because most social Darwinists favored white races.

15. D: The Japanese attack on Pearl Harbor was the turning point which caused the US to enter into World War II, even though the other events were all alarming to the US and caused them to give financial assistance to the Allies before officially entering the war on the Allies' side. A student might guess that the alliance between Japan, Germany, and Italy was the turning point because it involves Japan becoming an Axis power, but it was the actual attack on Pearl Harbor which led to America entering the war.

16. B: Germany and Japan both had scientists working on nuclear bombs, and one of Project Trinity's most important goals was to make sure that the US developed a bomb first and could thereby win the war through superior technology. Italy was not yet working on atomic bombs. A student might pick choice D because the excerpt mentions New Mexico and potential Japanese enemies, but that is incorrect. Choice A is also incorrect as the development of nuclear energy was not the goal of Project Trinity.

17. A: The "French coastline" is a clue that the Normandy Invasion is the correct answer, although a student may think "Bulge" or "Midway" is located in France. The high number of troops, ships, and aircraft is another clue that the facts describe D-Day. But a student not familiar with all of the other battles in World War II may pick one of the incorrect answers.

18. B: A main purpose of Victory Gardens was to decrease demand on commercial vegetable growers, thereby making more food available to soldiers. There were other purposes, such as providing nutritious foods to all people (not just poor immigrants) on the home front and boosting morale at home, but those were secondary and are not listed as answer choices. The other three answer choices listed are all incorrect.

19. C: The map's arrows show the routes the Berlin Airlift used to supply West Berlin with food supplies during a Soviet blockade. It does not show a bombing route, a route for moving captured German airplanes, or a route for tourists.

20. B: While all the titles have a connection of some kind to at least one or two items on the given list, choice B provides the BEST title for the list to show what all the items have in common: reasons for US involvement in the Korean War. The policy of containment may have been partially effective, because Korea was only one country falling to communism. The United Nations item would probably not fall under a title about containment, McCarthyism, or the HUAC committee, because those were all more internal to the US only. The U.N. was encouraging nations to get involved in the Korean War, so it fits under that title.

21. B: When Nixon referred to a "silent majority," he meant Americans who supported the Vietnam War but were not overly expressive about their opinions, unlike certain loud war protestors. The other options all relate to Americans and their relations to or opinions about the Vietnam War, but none of those are correct answers for the meaning of a "silent majority."

22. C: While the 13th and 14th Amendments granted important freedom from slavery and citizenship to African Americans, it was the 15th Amendment, a voting rights amendment, which made it possible for African Americans to elect each other as representatives by voting in large numbers. The 19th Amendment was also a voting rights amendment, but for women, and after the time period described in the excerpt.

23. B: This item tests the student's knowledge of armed forces desegregation AND the student's ability to read a chart. Reading the chart correctly and knowing general civil rights history will tell the student that choice B is correct. African Americans started making up a larger percentage of Staff Sergeant or Petty Officer Ranks in the Army, Navy, and Marines. If the student reads the type of officer rank incorrectly on the chart, he or she might pick choice A. The percentage of African-American staff sergeants and petty officers in the Navy did not increase as much as in the Army or

Marines, so a student might pick C, but there was still a slight increase, making choice C incorrect. Choice D is incorrect if the student understands the "years" columns in the charts.

24. C: It is the only choice that states what constituted illegal activities because they violated an arms embargo that was in place against Iran, and was an illegal diversion of funds. Weapons were illegally sold to Iran by the US government. Funds from the arms sales were illegally diverted to support the Contras, a group fighting the Nicaraguan government. The other answer choices offer incorrect variations on these statements, or confuse the fact that Contras were against and not inside the Nicaraguan government.

25. D: The "War on Terror" is the correct terminology. "Homeland Radicalism" takes some words from the excerpt but does not describe how the US was combating terrorism. The Persian Gulf War may have been one part of the War on Terror, but it does not include homeland security measures. The phrase "Terrorism Crisis" may have been used by the media or government at some point, but not as often as "War on Terror."

26. C: The excerpt gives information that Muhlenberg was a reverend and then a colonel in the Continental Army (as shown by his revealing of a Revolutionary colonel's uniform). The third correct choice is that he was one of the members of the first US Congress, which the student should know from general social studies knowledge (as it is not in the excerpt). Or at least the student could use process of elimination to eliminate some of the other incorrect answers that claim he was first Governor of Connecticut or Virginia, a signer of the Declaration of Independence, or a British Army member.

27. A: The Chinese Exclusion Act of 1882 was passed for the purpose of banning Chinese immigrants from the United States. Students with knowledge of social issues affecting immigrants during that time period will know this answer. Choices C and D (prohibiting Chinese Americans from working on railroads or settling in the west) were probably secondary purposes of the act, but were not written into the legislation as choice A was.

28. A: Choices C and D are good guesses, because Amelia Earhart was the first female solo pilot, but Lindbergh did not train her. His son was kidnapped and it did lead to the law passed by Congress, but not until the mid-late 1930s. He was also not the first solo pilot across the Pacific in the 1920s. Choice A is correct: He was the first solo pilot to fly nonstop across the Atlantic Ocean in 1927.

29. B: The Navajo Code Talkers were the US Marines group in World War II that used this code to save lives. The other choices all sound like reasonable alternatives, because tanks and dive bombers were used in World War I and II, and Sioux and Navajo were both American-Indian tribes at the time. Also, the term "code" appears in all four answer choices. But a student with general social studies knowledge at this grade level should know that B is the correct answer.

30. D: The Cuban Missile Crisis is the more famous name for the "13 Days in October" in which President John F. Kennedy played an important role. It is also sometimes called "World at the Brink," which may cause students to incorrectly choose answer B. It was a crisis involving fears of communism, which could lead students to incorrectly pick choice C. There was nuclear danger, and the Dominican Republic is another island in the Caribbean near the coast of America, which could lead students to incorrectly pick choice A. Their general knowledge of social studies at this grade level should lead to the correct choice of D.

31. A: Like the Native Americans of the Great Plains, white settlers also came to rely on buffalo for food and for providing warm robes on cold nights. The student needs to read the excerpt closely to understand that there were other uses for buffalo besides just food. A student who does not read the excerpt closely might pick choice C if he or she associated deer and elk with sleigh-riding, as many people do. A student might pick choice B if he or she considers that none of the animals listed are dangerous, though that could be a misreading because coyote, bear, and sometimes even buffalo and elk could be dangerous to settlers.

32. B: While it might be easier to buy supplies after the long hike through Chilkoot Pass, the fact was that miners would have to buy their supplies in the biggest city, Juneau, before making the rest of the trip. Also, some choices can be eliminated based on the fact that there does not seem to be a lot happening on the map at Yukon Hills or 40 miles into the Dominion of Canada. So choice B is the correct answer, which students can determine from the map, the arrows on the map, the collection of mining camps around the Klondike River, and their general knowledge of social studies: miners buy supplies in Juneau, steamboats carry them from Juneau to Ty-a, they pack their loads and hike through Chilkoot Pass, and they take boats down Lewis River to the Klondike River.

33. A: Choice D sounds possibly correct because the Senator is concluding that Panama is a superior location for a canal, but he notes that there actually were a few earthquakes in Panama, so it can't be said that there were never earthquakes in Panama. Choice A is correct that earthquake and volcano dangers to canals had to be considered when picking a location for a canal. Panama was chosen over Nicaragua because it had less earthquake risk and no volcano risk.

34. C: The excerpt gives a summary of Causes of the Great Migration. A student should know from general social studies knowledge that the Great Migration refers to movements of African Americans from southern states to states in the Northern, Western, and Midwestern United States. The excerpt gives the reasons why African Americans would make such a move. A student might pick answer A because of mention of the South (if not reading closely), or might pick the other choices for mention of migration or expansion, but only C is correct.

35. A: The fact that immigrants tended in the 1990s to settle in port-of-entry states means that, for US demographics, there would be a high number of immigrants settling in states such as California, New York, and Texas. Colorado, Utah, and Nebraska are not typical port-of-entry states (even though they do have airports). The fact given does not provide any implication that native-born Americans would flee from states where new immigrants are settling. However, there is also no reason to think that there would be zero demographic effect from an influx of new immigrants, making choices C and D incorrect.

36. A: A positive impact of Tin Pan Alley was that it was the birthplace of American popular music and created the ASCAP (American Society of Composers, Authors, and Publishers). A negative about Tin Pan Alley and ASCAP was that it was a predominantly white group for many years until the late 1920s, when the popularity of blues and jazz music by African–American musicians gained them admittance into the ASCAP. For all the other choices, the positive impact listed is correct. But the negative impacts listed are all incorrect, thus making those choices all incorrect. Composers did become rich from Tin Pan Alley; the location is no longer a hub of music publishing companies today as it once was; and they did give jobs to many new immigrants, especially Jewish and Russian immigrants in NYC.

37. D: All of the items on the list represent American Pop Culture Influences on the World. Many of the list items do have headquarters in California, but McDonald's has its headquarters in Illinois. Some of the things began in the 1920s or 30s, but not all of them, so those answer choices would also be incorrect.

38. B: The illustration best shows an example of the Americanization Movement to Assimilate Native Americans into American Culture. There may have been a battle between Native Americans and white settlers before or after this illustration, but that is not shown in the picture. Native Americans did not tend to be evangelicals; rather, the white settlers were evangelical about converting Native Americans to their religion. The picture also does not detail the move of Native Americans to reservations, although that also could have become before or after the illustration shown.

39. B: Based on the fact that the excerpt mentions Hull House, and information is given that the woman was a famous social worker in Chicago in the early 1900s, the student should be able to figure out that Jane Addams is the correct answer. Dr. Jacobs was a Dutch suffragette leader who invited Addams to some international projects with her. Susan B. Anthony was also a suffragette, but in the US and around the same time period as Addams. Frances Willard was a social reformer whose work was all done in the 1800s.

40. C: Dolores Huerta won the Outstanding Labor Leader Award from the state of California in 1984 recognizing her lifetime of work with Cesar Chavez on behalf of migrant farm workers. Gloria Anzaldua was a poet and cultural critic. Isabel Allende is a fiction writer from Chile. Sonia Sotomayor is a Supreme Court Justice.

41. C: The correct translation of *E Pluribus Unum* is "Out of Many, One." "In God We Trust" was adopted as the official motto of the US later in history. "In Union We Trust" might be a good guess because "Unum" sounds like it could be a Latin version of "Union." "The many are united" also sounds like a plausible translation for *E Pluribus Unum*, even though it is actually incorrect.

42. B: The fact that Baker fought in Italy is a clue that either WWI or WWII is the correct answer, and that both the Korean War and Vietnam War would be incorrect, even though there was still some racial prejudice during the times of those wars. The fact that President Clinton presented Baker with the award gives a clue that it must have been for fighting during WWII, as Baker would probably not have been old enough to fight in WWI and still be alive under President Clinton's years. In fact, a student could deduce that, if Baker was 78 years old in 1997 that would mean he was born in 1919, which was after WWI. Also, general social studies knowledge suggests that students know who Vernon J. Baker is for this grade level.

43. C: The New Deal programs gave state and federal governments increased power to affect the economy. They did not take power away from the federal government. The programs did not need Supreme Court approval to be passed, because Congress passed the New Deal. And it was also not the first time that legislation affected farmers, because there was a Federal Farm Loan act in 1916, and other laws before the mid-1930s that probably affected farmers.

44. A: The Ethics in Government Act of 1978 was enacted after the Watergate Scandal of the early 1970s had eroded some public trust in government officials. The Teapot Dome Scandal occurred much earlier in the century, not in the 1960s. Newspapers were also not making up stories about unethical government officials, but they were reporting on Watergate. It is true that Gerald Ford did not get re-elected, partly because he was unpopular for pardoning Nixon, but not because he was considered unethical. Ford was not the impetus for the Ethics Act.

45. A: Providing increased border controls on the Canada-US border was part of the USA PATRIOT Act of 2001 and affected the private and public sectors of people traveling between those two countries. The other choices listed all sound like they could be related to interactions between the US and Canada. For example, lawful commerce in arms could relate to guns sold between countries, but it was for guns within the United States. A Trade Act might apply to US-Canada trade, but not to border patrols. The "Fence" Act applied to the Mexico-US border, not the Canada-US border.

46. C: The U.N. has been a leader in helping end the crisis in Darfur, which helps the US and its international image when it participates in the U.N. The other choices are all false statements. The U.N. does get involved in deadly conflicts, civil wars, and aid for victims of natural disasters. The U.N. also generally does have the same foreign policy objectives as the US

47. D: This case marked the first time that the judicial branch of government involved itself in a federal election, and critics said that the Supreme Court rather than the electorate had determined the winner of a presidential election. There may have been some changes in the way states did recounts, but that is not the BEST description of the historical importance of the case. Choice B is incorrect because there had been other Supreme Court cases with president's names in them, such as *US v. Nixon* in 1974, and likely several others too. Also, presidential candidates had probably been hiring lawyers even before campaigns started, long before that year's election.

48. D: Southern opponents of segregation used intimidation and violence against desegregation proponents, and many southern school districts avoided compliance with the new law. The President eventually did have to call in National Guard troops to help with desegregation, but that was a few years later. The Cold War may have started in the 1950s, but did not draw complete attention away from segregation issues.

49. D: Choice A sounds like a good guess, but choice D is the correct answer. Before the *White v. Regester* Supreme Court case, Texas had an "at large" voting system that had weakened minority voting power. The new voting from individual districts would allow more equal representation for heavily Hispanic voting districts, allowing them to have more Hispanic representatives. Choice C would not be correct because the poll tax was outlawed many years before the 1973 case.

50. B: Andrew Carnegie was a wealthy industrialist who, both alone and in cooperation with John Rockefeller, gave money to schools, universities, libraries, and former employees, starting the modern practice of corporate philanthropy in the early 1900s. Henry Ward Beecher was a leader who encouraged wealthy men to donate money to good causes around the same time period. John Stuart Mill was also a contemporary of Carnegie and encouraged donations for education. Elbert H. Gary was Carnegie's partner in a steel company, but not the main impetus behind philanthropic donations. So Andrew Carnegie is the correct answer, and the excerpt is from Carnegie's autobiography.

51. B: Students who know the meaning of "right to habeas corpus" will know that it means the right to be brought before a court, which was unconstitutionally denied to Japanese Americans in internment camps during World War II. The other options are all rights which were also violated against Japanese Americans in camps, but not in this particular example of not getting a court date. A student who does not know the meaning of *habeas corpus* may be able to use process of elimination about the other rights (although they may confuse "assembling" with going to a court, or confuse "involuntary servitude" with camp "imprisonment") in order to get the correct answer.

52. D: Payments to senators were not a method used by suffragettes trying to get the 19th Amendment allowing women the right to vote passed. They did use all of the other methods, however, such as speeches, writing articles, nonviolent protesting, and marching.

53. D: It is the best description of what laissez-faire economists believed, which is that marketplace forces were enough to regulate businesses. In contrast, most Progressives wanted more trust-busting laws and federal, state, and local government intervention to help regulate businesses that were perhaps producing unsafe products, forming monopolies to drive up prices, or taking advantage of working people.

54. B: The Interstate Commerce Act of 1887 provided for all the measures listed in the table, although not all were able to be completely enforced. Reading the list carefully and having a general knowledge of social studies and US history should lead students to the correct answers, although a student could mistakenly pick one of the other choices listed for their connection to railways, dollars, or Federal Reserve money. (Dollar Diplomacy was a strategy, not an actual piece of legislation.)

55. B: It is the BEST summary for what President Warren Harding meant by a "Return to Normalcy." He was calling for a return to peaceful times and a focus on domestic issues, as opposed to a focus on international war. Choice A is a good guess because the president would want a good economy, and industry had been busy during WWI before falling off slightly after the war. But choice B is the best answer. He was not calling for going out in search of more territories or for higher immigration rates.

56. A: Herbert Hoover addressed bank failures in his 1930 State of the Union address because bank failures were one of the primary causes of the Great Depression. Congress eventually did want to start a Federal Deposit Insurance Program to help insure banks against future bank failures, but that was the 1933 Congress and Franklin Roosevelt, not the 1930 Congress and Herbert Hoover.

57. B: Herbert Hoover was a main opponent of the New Deal, for the reason listed in this answer choice. The New Deal programs were passed by the 1933 Congress and again in 1935 Congress for the "Second Hundred Days" of New Deal programs. The New Deal programs proved to be popular with the American public, who overwhelmingly re-elected FDR for his second term as President, so choice A is incorrect.

58. D: It best fills in the blank space on the chart, explaining how the FDIC originally worked in the 1930s: "Provided deposit insurance to banks and had the authority to regulate and supervise banks." Seeing the chart's statement of how the FDIC still works today should give students a clue to the correct answer. The FDIC did not give gold to banks, although gold was stored and Fort Knox was built in the 1930s. A student might choose C for its mention of "insurance," but that was not the kind of insurance provided by the FDIC. Also, the FDIC was supposed to prevent customer runs on banks, not encourage them.

59. C: It gives the BEST explanation of a cause and an effect of the decrease in unemployment during WWII. Choice C states "Cause: Wartime economic boom expanded industrial production, with less workforce competition due to need for wartime soldiers. Effect: Helped end the Great Depression." Those are both true statements related to decreased unemployment during the war. All the other choices give false causes and effects. Choice D gives a cause that is really an effect of the decrease in unemployment (that women and minorities could more easily be hired).

60. A: While an argument could be made that choice B is also correct, there was not a phenomenon actually named the "Women Quitting Work Effect," so choice A is the BEST choice for describing the phenomenon illustrated by the given statistic. The statistic shows the post war Baby Boom, and its effect was to increase the economy and consumer demand for products. Choice D describes the opposite of a Baby Boom, so it is not correct, and choice C was not a historical phenomenon.

61. C: All the programs listed were part of President Lyndon B. Johnson's Great Society programs. The students' general knowledge of social studies should place most of those programs within the 1960s time period, making Presidents Kennedy or Johnson the best guesses. But because many of the programs do not have to do with civil rights, Johnson becomes the best guess for a student to make over the other choices provided.

62. D: The result of OPEC's oil embargo on the US free enterprise system was inflation, economic recession, and restrictions on gasoline purchases; and auto manufacturers making smaller and more fuel-efficient cars. US auto manufacturers may have sold cars to Europe also, but Europe was also targeted by OPEC's embargo. Choices A and C are also incorrect.

63. B: While all the entrepreneurs listed are also philanthropic donors, and have at times been considered one of the richest men in the world, the mention of "computer industry" will be a clue to most students with basic social studies/current events knowledge that Bill Gates is the correct answer.

64. D: The stock ticker and the telegraph could be related to the information in this excerpt because they were ways for businessmen to relay information to each other, as described in the excerpt. However, the astute student will see that the excerpt describes businessmen talking to each other, therefore the excerpt is describing the benefits of the telephone invention. A student might pick choice A, coal smelting, if they only focus on the first sentence of the excerpt about the coal company foreman.

65. A: It can BEST be made based on the timeline facts. Historical events and the specific needs of society can contribute to medical inventions, such as how the history of polio outbreaks and the fact that a President had the disease contributed to the scientific discovery of a polio vaccine. The other statements cannot be proven true by the timeline facts. Other countries besides the US also had polio outbreaks in the 1920s and 1930s. Disease outbreaks can sometimes be prevented in other ways besides just from vaccines. And it was Jonas Salk, not FDR, who invented the polio vaccine, although FDR helped raise money to fund scientific research.

66. C: It is the BEST inference that can be made based on the excerpt, which discusses the new assembly line method that Ford used in factories and how it increased the productivity of workers. The development of the assembly line method in factories led to increased worker productivity. The increased productivity can be inferred from the discussion of "convenience" and lessening steps. The excerpt does not discuss time-study analysis (at least not as much as assembly lines, even if some mention of time is included), and does not discuss inventory management as much. It does not describe Ford working on the assembly line alongside his employees. While there is some mention of ergonomics (having men not have to stoop, for example), it is not the main focus of the excerpt, so would not be the BEST inference to make. Also, it could be bad ergonomics for workers to not take many steps and to repeat the same movements over and over on assembly lines.

67. A: It is the BEST summary of the facts presented in the timeline, which are that technologies used in space explorations can also improve the quality of life on Earth. It is a good suggestion that doctors and architects study space technologies, but just naming one of those professions does not summarize the whole timeline, because only one fact deals with architectural use of space technologies, and using the doctor choice as a summary leaves out the architectural use. Choice D may be a true statement, but because there is no mention of the cost of space exploration in the timeline, it is not a good summary of the timeline.

68. A: Students who know enough about North American Trade and the recent US policy of involvement in such trade will know that NAFTA was started in 1994 and is the correct answer. The other three options sound like plausible replacements if a US-Canada Free Trade Agreement was being replaced, but they are not real organizations and so they are not correct answers.

Practice Test #2

Use the chart and your knowledge of social studies to answer the following question:

ERA in US History	Approximate Dates	Defining Characteristics of this Era
Gilded Age or Progressive Era	1890-1914	The era was called "gilded" because of expanded wealth and prosperity. "Progressive" describes the politics of the time that called for social reforms and eliminating corruption in government.
World War I Era	1914-1918	The US was involved in fighting a war in Europe.
Roaring Twenties	1918-1928	
Great Depression	1929-1940	
World War II Era	1941-1945	
Cold War Era	1945-1964	

1. Which defining characteristic listed below should go in the row for describing the Roaring Twenties Era?

a. After a World War, America wanted to help rebuild Europe and prevent the Soviet Union's possible expansion of communism.
b. After the stock market crash, many businesses failed and unemployment became high.
c. The US was involved in fighting a war with Allies against Germany, Japan, and Italy.
d. The economy was strong with a great demand for new products, while culture in this era, also known as the "Jazz Age," became more experimental.

2. Which Founding Father was governor of Connecticut during and after the Revolutionary War, and was the only governor of a British colony who sided with colonists during the Revolutionary War?

a. Charles Carroll
b. Benjamin Rush
c. Jonathan Trumbull
d. John Witherspoon

Use the map and your knowledge of social studies to answer the following question:

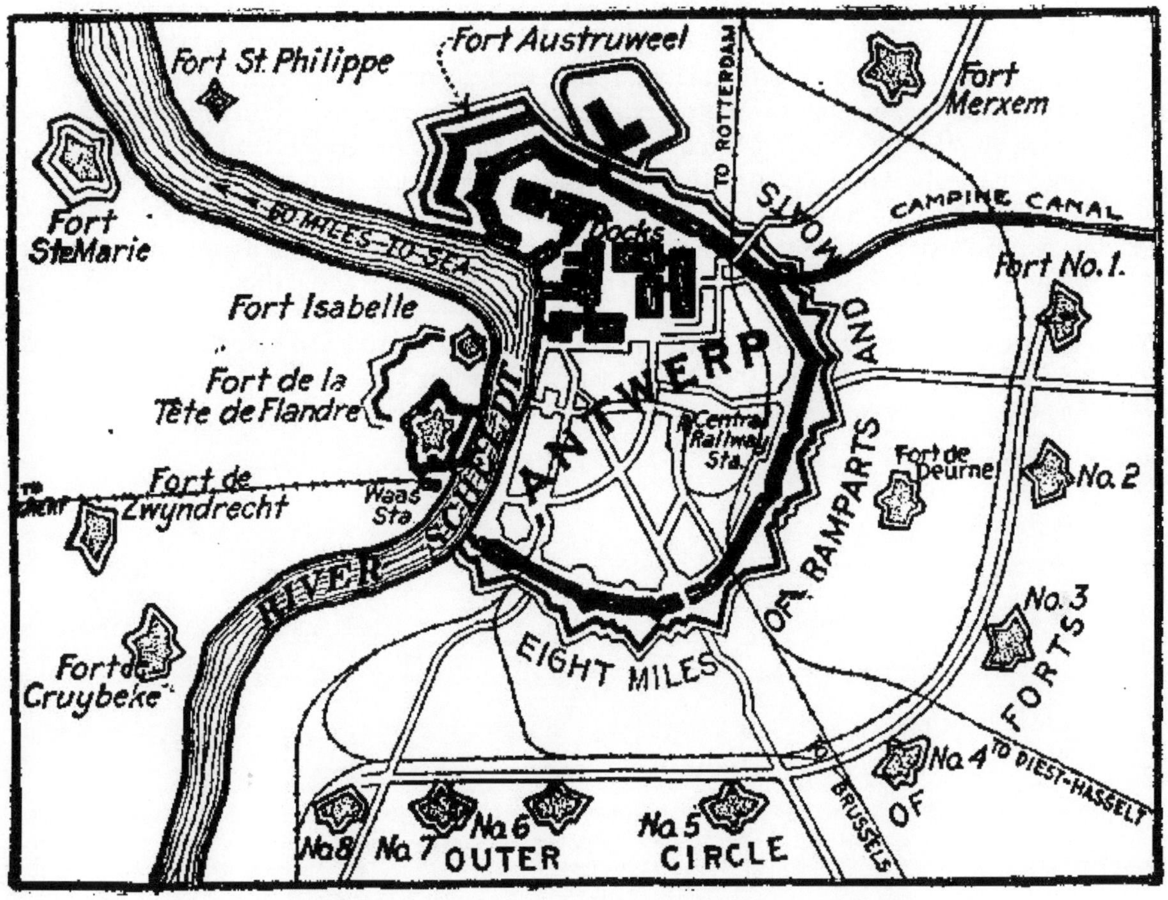

ANTWERP AND ITS FORTIFICATIONS

3. Why was the city of Antwerp in Belgium so heavily fortified in 1914?

a. World War I had started; Germany had invaded other Belgian cities and was going to invade Antwerp also.
b. World War I had started; Italy had invaded other Belgian cities and was going to invade Antwerp also.
c. Antwerp was fortifying against British air attacks that might take place during World War I.
d. Antwerp feared a Russian invasion after the start of World War I.

4. Which choice below lists some contributions to early America made by John Jay?

a. He was the first Chief Justice of New York and also a Minister to France.
b. He signed the Declaration of Independence and was one of the first mayors of New York City.
c. He served in George Washington's army during the Revolution and was Minister to Spain after the war.
d. He was a foreign minister, a contributing writer to the Federalist Papers, and an early governor of New York.

Use the excerpt and your knowledge of social studies to answer the following question:

> "Perhaps the most characteristic feature of this record of lynch law for the year 1893, is the remarkable fact that five human beings were lynched and that the matter was considered of so little importance that the powerful press bureaus of the country did not consider the matter of enough importance to ascertain the causes for which they were hanged. It tells the world, with perhaps greater emphasis than any other feature of the record, that Lynch Law has become so common in the United States that the finding of the dead body of a Negro, suspended between heaven and earth to the limb of a tree, is of so slight importance that neither the civil authorities nor press agencies consider the matter worth investigating."

5. The above excerpt comes from a book written by a female African-American "muckraker" journalist and reform leader in 1895. What was this author's name?

a. Ella Baker
b. Rosa Parks
c. Sojourner Truth
d. Ida B. Wells

Use the photograph, caption, and your knowledge of social studies to answer the following question:

German Air Raiders over England
In the foreground three British planes are advancing to the attack

6. Based on the photograph and caption from a book about World War I, and your general social studies knowledge, which statement below is MOST likely true?

a. The only airplane warfare during World War I occurred over England.
b. In World War I, American allies had better airplane technology than German allies.
c. Airplane warfare was used in the Civil War before being more widely used in World War I.
d. Airplanes had their first warfare use during World War I, at first just for taking spy photographs, and later for firing guns and dropping bombs.

Use the excerpt and your knowledge of social studies to answer the following question:

In *The Great Round World and What Is Going On In It*, a weekly magazine, Sanford B. Dole was interviewed in 1898 about the US plan to annex Hawaii:

> "President Dole made a glowing picture of the benefits that this country would receive from annexation. It would greatly encourage commerce between the United

States and Hawaii by making the trade absolutely free, and it would open up to Americans a great many industries, the chief among them being coffee-growing.

"It would also vastly improve the condition of the islands themselves.

In case annexation is rejected by our Government, President Dole says the Hawaiian Government will continue much as it is at present."

7. What was Sanford B. Dole the president of in 1898?

a. The Republic of Hawaii
b. The State of Hawaii
c. The United States
d. The United States Senate

Use the list and your knowledge of social studies to answer the following question:

- It proved that the US was willing to expand its empire and gain resources through imperialism (the taking of colonies).
- It allowed the US to annex Guam, Hawaii, Puerto Rico, and the Philippines.
- It showed the power and strength of the US army and navy.

8. What would be the BEST summarizing title for this list?

a. How the Policies of President Theodore Roosevelt Made the US a World Power
b. How the Spanish-American War Helped the US Become a World Power
c. How the War of 1812 Helped the US Become a World Power
d. How Isolationism Led to Imperialism for the US

Use the excerpt and your knowledge of social studies to answer the following question:

President Woodrow Wilson's "Fourteen Points" speech in 1918 included the following lines:

"XIV. A general association of nations must be formed under specific covenants for the purpose of affording mutual guarantees of political independence and territorial integrity to great and small states alike.

"In regard to these essential rectifications of wrong and assertions of right we feel ourselves to be intimate partners of all the governments and peoples associated together against the Imperialists. We cannot be separated in interest or divided in

9. Based on this excerpt, what was one way that Wilson's "Fourteen Points" contrasted with his pre-war position of US neutrality?

a. In 1918, Wilson agreed with the philosophy of the imperialists.
b. By 1918, Wilson thought that each nation should form its own government.
c. In this speech, Wilson believed that each nation should be able to decide its own territories.
d. In this speech, Wilson wanted to set up a League of Nations which would eventually become the United Nations.

10. Progressive Era reformers in the early 1900s wanted greater involvement by federal government in public affairs to improve schools, roads, parks, public health, farms, and more. Because government would need money for such reforms, which amendment did Progressives help pass that allowed income tax collection?

a. 16th Amendment
b. 17th Amendment
c. 18th Amendment
d. 19th Amendment

Use the illustration and your knowledge of social studies to answer the following question:

A sketch from *I Was There...with the Yanks in France* by C. LeRoy Baldridge, written in 1919, shows a sketch of an old trench in the Argonne forest of France

11. Why was the Battle of the Argonne Forest in 1918 difficult and important?

a. The battle was difficult because there was no air support available to the Allies during this time and important because the Allies won anyway.
b. The battle was difficult because there were many Allied prisoners of war hidden in the trenches who needed to be rescued and important because the prisoners were rescued.
c. The battle was difficult because of the deeply forested nature of the area and important because it was the last battle won by the Germans before the end of World War I.
d. The battle was difficult because the Germans were so entrenched in this forest, having built deep trenches there, and important because it was one of the final battles of the war and helped break through Germany's western front.

12. In the Progressive Era of the late 1890s and early 1900s, political reformers wanted to make sure government represented the peoples' will. An "initiative" process began in 1898 in South Dakota and then spread to other states. Which definition BEST describes the initiative process?

a. It allowed voting citizens to give their judgment on proposed legislation before state legislators voted on the same legislation.
b. It allowed voters to gather petitions demanding special elections when they wanted to recall an unpopular public official, thereby allowing them to "un-elect" that official.
c. It allowed citizens to introduce legislation proposals at a local or state level by gathering petitions, and proposals would then be addressed by lawmakers or placed on ballots for a vote.
d. It allowed citizens to visit state legislatures and give testimony supporting a certain issue, thereby encouraging the state lawmakers to propose and pass legislation on that same issue.

13. An "Emergency Quota Law" in 1921 was signed by the president to limit new immigrants to the US was most likely an effect of which popular philosophy of the time period?

a. Harlem Renaissance, which showed that African Americans had much to contribute to society and should be given jobs before letting in more immigrants.
b. Nativism, a belief that native-born Americans, especially white Americans, were superior to foreign-born Americans.
c. Prohibition, a belief that alcohol was un-American because beer was mostly brewed by German-Americans, and thus immigration of Germans and other Europeans with alcohol as part of their cultural traditions should be limited.
d. Women's Suffrage Movement, arguing that women should get rights before more immigrants were let in the US

Use the timeline and your knowledge of social studies to answer the following question:

Dec. 7, 1941 - Pearl Harbor in Hawaii is bombed by Japan. The FBI arrests some Japanese-American community leaders who are held away from their families.

Dec. 8, 1941 - US Congress declares war on Japan.

Feb. 19, 1942 - President Franklin D. Roosevelt signs Executive Order 9066, ordering military areas off-limits to certain people.

March 18, 1942 - President Roosevelt signs Executive Order 9102, which establishes a "War Relocation Authority."

14. What event would BEST go next in this timeline's factual sequence of events?

a. Thousands of Japanese-American men, women and children are relocated from the US west coast for east coast locations.
b. All Japanese-American men are denied the chance to be US soldiers for the duration of World War II.
c. Thousands of Japanese-American men, women and children are relocated to internment camps.
d. Many Japanese-American men have their passports confiscated and are forced to leave the US

15. In May 1991, the First International Gathering of Children Hidden during World War II held a meeting in New York City. Around 1,600 former hidden children attended this meeting. Which of the following is the BEST explanation for why these adults had to be hidden as children in Europe during World War II?

a. They were in danger of being drafted into youth army groups in fascist Germany.
b. They were hiding from war zones and waiting for fake passports to take them to Israel.
c. They had to be hidden from French families who would have taken them away from their original homelands to adopt them.
d. They were Jewish and had to be hidden from Nazis in order to survive the Holocaust, the attempted extermination of the Jewish population by Nazi Germany.

Use the photo and your knowledge of social studies to answer the following question:

Damage Inspection: A squadron operations officer of the 332d Fighter Group points out a cannon hole to ground crew, Italy, 1945

16. Besides being called the "332nd Fighter Group," what was another name for those fighter pilots in World War II?

a. Flying Tigers
b. Red Barons
c. Top Guns
d. Tuskegee Airmen

17. Why did the North Atlantic Treaty Organization (NATO) form with a military alliance between the US and several European countries in 1949?

a. It formed to defend against communist Soviet Union which had taken over some central and eastern European countries.
b. It formed to combine with the work of the United Nations in policing war-ravaged areas of the third world.
c. NATO formed to combat international terrorism and regulate nuclear weapons.
d. NATO formed to defend against a re-united Germany.

18. The "Domino Theory," first suggested by President Dwight Eisenhower but also followed by presidents after him, claimed that if one nation in Asia became a communist country, then other Asian countries would follow soon afterwards, like a set of dominoes. The US fought a war in which country because of this theory?

a. Burma
b. China
c. Thailand
d. Vietnam

19. By autumn of 1967, 93 percent of American homes had a television. Most of the evening news was reporting about the Vietnam War, and about 50 million Americans watched the news each night. What was an effect of these media developments?

a. The views of war action inspired many men to register for the draft.
b. Positive media coverage of the war's progress resulted in an increase of American support for the war.
c. News with graphic images and interviews with frustrated soldiers resulted in a decrease of American public support for the war.
d. Although Walter Cronkite, a trusted television news anchor, supported the US staying in the war, Americans started to decide it was not a good idea to stay in Vietnam.

20. Which social activist helped start a union for workers' rights in 1962 called the *National Farm Workers Association* (NFWA)?

a. Cesar Chavez
b. Felix Longoria
c. Hector P. Garcia
d. Martin Luther King, Jr.

Use the excerpt and your knowledge of social studies to answer the following question:

Excerpt from *The Black Experience in America* by Norman Coombs, 1972:

"In November [of 1963], Congressional debate on the Civil Rights Bill was still continuing, but the President had now made the passage of the Civil Rights Bill one of the most urgent goals of his Administration. But on the 22nd of November, John F. Kennedy was gunned down in the Presidential limousine in Dallas, Texas. The nation and the world were struck dumb with disbelief. Even those who had disliked his politics were horrified at the assassination of a President in a democratic state. His supporters felt that they had lost a friend as well as a leader...

The sense of shock caused despair and gloom. The fact that his successor, Lyndon B. Johnson, was a Southerner led most civil rights supporters to feel that there would be a reversal of federal policies on the racial question. However, Johnson immediately tried to reassure the nation that his intention was to carry on with the unfinished business of the Kennedy era."

21. Based on this excerpt and your knowledge of social studies, what could be predicted would happen next in history?

a. President Johnson did sign a Civil Rights Act, but not until 1967.
b. Congress passed a Civil Rights Act in 1964, and President Johnson signed it.
c. Congress passed a Civil Rights Act in 1964, but President Johnson did not sign it.
d. Without the leadership of President Kennedy, congress did not pass a Civil Rights Act until the 1970s.

Use the chart and your knowledge of social studies to answer the following question:

Participants	Date	Agreements Made
Israeli Prime Minister Menachem Begin (signer)	1979	Israel agreed to return the Sinai to Egypt
Egyptian President Anwar el-Sadat (signer)		Egypt and Israel agreed to work on Palestinian independence steps for the West Bank and Gaza
US President Jimmy Carter (Witness)		

22. What would be the BEST title for this chart?

a. Arab Spring Agreements
b. Camp David Accords
c. Palestine Liberation Organization Treaty
d. Peace through Strength Plans

Use the excerpt and your knowledge of social studies to answer the following question:

Excerpt from *The Black Experience in America* by Norman Coombs, 1972

"He held that, when the rights of blacks were violated, they should be willing to die in the struggle to secure them:

"If white America doesn't think the Afro-American, especially the upcoming generation, is capable of adopting the guerrilla tactics now being used by oppressed people elsewhere on this earth, she is making a drastic mistake. She is underestimating the force that can do her the most harm.

"A real honest effort to remove the just grievances of the 22 million Afro-Americans must be made immediately or in a short time it will be too late."

"The slogan 'Black Power' exploded from a public address system in Greenwood, Mississippi, in the summer of 1966..."

23. Which historical figure was MOST likely the speaker of the long quote in this excerpt (the one that starts "If white America...")?

a. James Meredith
b. Malcolm X
c. Martin Luther King, Jr.
d. William Clay

Use the list and your knowledge of social studies to answer the following question:

Jobs
Land
Political freedoms
Religious freedoms

24. What is the BEST explanation for what the items on this list all had in common during the late 1800s?

a. These were all promises of President Theodore Roosevelt's administration
b. These were all reasons why immigrants came to America in hopes of better lives
c. These were all reasons why settlers made a rush to California and other western states
d. These were all things offered by the government to Native Americans at that time period

Use the excerpt and your knowledge of social studies to answer the following question:

"The earnestness of the Americans in the situation was proclaimed to the world by the English and French, and General Pershing placed his name and that of his country and men high on the wall of fame by unselfishly offering to France at the most critical period the use of his entire force, to be disposed of and assigned wherever General Foch and his staff decided to use them. Within a few days thereafter the American troops which had been in training were marched in to relieve the stressed English and French."

25. The author of this excerpt is describing a turning point in which war?

a. War of 1812
b. Spanish-American War
c. World War I
d. World War II

26. Who headed the National Association for the Advancement of Colored People (NAACP) in 1910, founded and edited the NAACP's journal *The Crisis*, and wrote many "muckraking" articles for *The Crisis* about civil rights for African Americans?

a. W.E.B. DuBois
b. Matthew Gaines
c. Marcus Garvey
d. Booker T. Washington

27. Which reason or reasons BEST explain why the US Office of War Information included famous stars such as Ethel Merman in their radio broadcasts in the 1940s?

a. To build morale, raise spirits, and help convince women they needed to stay home while men went to war
b. To build morale, raise spirits, and help convince women to apply for wartime work
c. To convince women to buy tickets to Broadway shows to support the US economy during wartime
d. To convince women to buy movie tickets to support the US economy during wartime

Use the excerpt and your knowledge of social studies to answer the following question:

"As you know, I will soon be visiting the People's Republic of China and the Soviet Union. I go there with no illusions. We have great differences with both powers. We shall continue to have great differences. But peace depends on the ability of great powers to live together on the same planet despite their differences."

28. Which president gave this speech, as he was about to become the first US President to visit the communist People's Republic of China?

a. President John F. Kennedy
b. President Lyndon B. Johnson
c. President Richard M. Nixon
d. President Gerald R. Ford

29. What event in April 1975 meant that the Vietnam War was over and that South Vietnam would surrender to the communists, leading to the eventual reunification of the country under communist rule?

a. Fall of Saigon
b. Ho Chi Minh's death
c. My Lai Massacre
d. Tet Offensive

30. "Old enough to fight, old enough to vote" became a slogan for a youth voting rights movement after the World War II military draft age was lowered to 18, while 21 remained the minimum voting age. The Vietnam War draft brought more urgency to the youth voting rights movement and resulted in which amendment to lower the voting age to 18?

a. 24th Amendment
b. 25th Amendment
c. 26th Amendment
d. 27th Amendment

Use the list and your knowledge of social studies to answer the following question:

Poor agricultural practices

Years of drought

Lack of ground cover to hold soil in place

High winds on the plains

31. What would be the BEST title to summarize this list?

a. Causes of the 1935 Dust Bowl
b. Effects of the 1935 Dust Bowl
c. Issues for the 1970s Era Rust Belt
d. Issues for the 1970s Era Sun Belt

Use the excerpt and your knowledge of social studies to answer the following question:

Excerpt from *Crossing the Plains, Days of '57* by William Audley Maxwell, 1915

"We forded the Platte at a point something like one hundred and fifty miles westward from its confluence with the Missouri. There was no road leading into the river, nor any evidence of its having been crossed by any one at that place. We were informed that the bottom was of quicksand, and fording, therefore, dangerous. We tested it, by riding horses across. Contrary to our expectations, the bottom was found to be a surface of smooth sand, packed hard enough to bear up the wagons, when the movement was quick and continuous. A cut was made in the bank, to form a runway for passage of the wagons to the water's edge; and the whole train crossed the stream safely, with no further mishap than the wetting of a driver and the dipping of a wagon into a place deep enough to let water into the box. Fording the Platte consumed one entire day. We camped that night on the north shore."

32. Which statement BEST summarizes the main idea of the above paragraph describing geographic factors for settlers headed to the Great Plains?

a. Fording the Platte River in stage coach wagons was dangerous because wagons often got caught in quicksand
b. Fording the Platte River was believed to be dangerous, but it turned out to be quick and easy for stage coach wagons
c. Fording the Platte River was thought to be dangerous, but it turned out to be mostly time-consuming and a little inconvenient
d. After fording the Platte River, stage coach wagons could continue driving west or could stop and camp for a night by the shore of the river

Use the chart and your knowledge of social studies to answer the following question:

US Census Data

(All population figures are per 200,000 square miles of land area)

Date	Northeastern US Rural Areas	Northeastern US Urban Areas
1890	Population average of around 7.5 million	Population average of around 12.5 million
1930	Population average of around 11 million	Population average of around 30 million

33. Which conclusion is MOST likely true based on this US Census Data chart?

a. Rural to urban migration was a probable trend between the years 1890 and 1930.
b. Urban to rural migration was a probable pattern between the years 1890 and 1930.
c. Urban areas grew in population numbers but rural areas had a decreased population between 1890 and 1930.
d. Rural areas grew in population numbers but urban areas had a decreased population between 1890 and 1930.

Use the timeline and your knowledge of social studies to answer the following question:

1962 - The book "Silent Spring," by Rachel Carson, was published and soon became a bestseller. The book exposed the negative effects of pesticides on the environment in the US

1969 - President Nixon set up a Cabinet-level "Environmental Quality Council" as well as a "Citizens' Advisory Committee on Environmental Quality."

1970 - In February, President Nixon announced stronger federal programs to deal with water and air pollution.

1970 - In April that year, the first Earth Day was celebrated in the US by about 20 million Americans.

34. Based on this timeline, which event MOST likely took place in December of 1970?

a. Future Vice President Al Gore gave a report on global warming to his fellow college students
b. Vietnam War protests overshadowed the public concern for a healthy environment and the issue faded away for a while
c. President Nixon oversaw the establishment of the National Park System, setting aside lands for protection and public recreation
d. President Nixon oversaw the establishment of the Environmental Protection Agency to consolidate pollution control and environmental protection

35. "Sustainable development" is defined as development that meets the needs of the present while still making possible the ability of future generations to meet their needs. It takes into account environmental impacts and tries to minimize damage to the environment. Which reason BEST describes why there is a need for sustainable development?

a. The environment will always evolve to adapt to the needs of future generations
b. Future generations will not have as many scientists because education is deteriorating
c. Population growth has stabilized, but there are still future stresses on the environment such as global warming
d. The continued forecasted population growth can damage the environment with greater stresses on oceans, food supplies, and land

36. In the 1960s, "Beat Generation" member Allen Ginsberg worked with psychologist Timothy Leary to promote more widespread use of the drug LSD. What was an impact of this on American society?

a. More widespread use made the drug LSD more popular and it became a legal drug.
b. LSD was a legal drug until the 1980s "War on Drugs" made it an illegal substance.
c. Politicians were some people who experimented with LSD and it made them more open-minded about political issues.
d. While some people may have felt that LSD was psychologically helpful, many people experienced bad effects such as fear or psychosis from the drug, and the drug was and is still illegal.

Use the excerpt and your knowledge of social studies to answer the following question:

In this excerpt from *The Black Experience in America* (1972), author Norman Coombs describes the 1920s Harlem Renaissance:

"Students, peasants, artists, businessmen, professional men, poets, musicians, and workers; all came to Harlem...Langston Hughes, in describing his first entrance into Harlem from the 135th Street subway exit, said that he felt vitality and hope throbbing in the air. In Black Manhattan, James Weldon Johnson said that Harlem was not a slum or a fringe. Rather, he insisted that it was one of the "most beautiful and healthful sections of the city."

37. Based on the excerpt, what was one probable impact of the Harlem Renaissance for African-American society?

a. It made African Americans feel like they were relegated to a ghetto culture
b. It gave African Americans a new sense of pride and confidence in their culture
c. The Harlem Renaissance made black people feel like they should only live in the Harlem area of Manhattan and not in any other cities
d. The Harlem Renaissance was helpful for black artists, musicians, and writers, but not for businessmen or other professional black people

Use the list and your knowledge of social studies to answer the following question:

- Islamic rap groups in England and France
- A Basque group in Spain called Negu Gorriak that incorporates US hip-hop
- Musicians in New Zealand who combine rap, soul and reggae with traditional Maori music

38. What is the BEST generalization that could be made based on this list?

a. American culture can spread globally through entertainment such as rap and hip-hop music, but that same culture sometimes gets reconstituted into new forms in other countries
b. Rap and hip-hop music have spread from the US to Spain, England, France, and New Zealand, but not to any other countries
c. Rap and hip-hop music are examples of ways that Hollywood influences culture in other countries
d. Rap and hip-hop music arose originally in other countries before becoming popular in the US

39. Which choice BEST shows the contributions of Italian-American women to US culture in the field of politics?

a. Sylvia Scaramelli helped co-found a college in New Jersey in 1942; Suzette Charles (born Suzette De Gaetano) was the first Italian American to win the Miss America title
b. The first woman to run for Vice President of the United States was Geraldine Ferraro in 1984; the first woman elected governor in her own right was Ella T. Grasso of Connecticut in 1975
c. Jerre Mangione wrote about the history of Italian Americans; Dr. Rosemarie Truglio studied the effects of television on children and teenagers
d. Sonia Sotomayor is a current female Supreme Court Justice; Don DeLillo is an Italian-American author

40. In which movement were members of the Quaker religious group NOT very active?

a. Abolitionist movement
b. McCarthyism movement
c. Pacifist and peace activist movements
d. Women's rights movement

41. Which First Lady was honorary vice chair of the Red Cross and led blood donation and fundraising drives during a war?

a. Edith Bolling Galt Wilson
b. Eleanor Roosevelt
c. Lady Bird Johnson
d. Pat Nixon

42. More than one elementary school in Texas is named after Roy Benavidez, a Mexican American born in Texas, and he was buried with full military honors at Fort Sam Houston National Cemetery. Why?

a. He was the first Mexican American to serve in the army and become a state senator in Texas
b. He was the first Mexican American to become a high-ranking officer in the army in the 1950s
c. He won a Congressional Medal of Honor for his brave military service during the Korean War
d. He won a Congressional Medal of Honor and a Purple Heart for his brave military service and actions in the Vietnam War

43. When the FBI examined homes of Japanese Americans without warrants during World War II, which constitutional right of those Japanese Americans was violated?

a. Right to reasonable bail
b. Freedom of the press
c. Freedom from unreasonable searches and seizures
d. Right to a speedy and public trial

44. How did all Native Americans achieve US citizenship?

a. By marrying white American citizens
b. By serving in American military units
c. By studying for and passing a citizenship test
d. Through passage of the American Indian Citizenship Act of 1924

Use the excerpt and your knowledge of social studies to answer the following question:

Excerpt from *Integration of the Armed Forces, 1940-1965*, by Morris J. MacGregor, Jr.

"The laws of 1866 and 1869 that guaranteed the existence of four black Regular Army regiments also institutionalized segregation, granting federal recognition to a system racially separate and theoretically equal in treatment and opportunity a generation before the Supreme Court sanctioned such a distinction in *Plessy* v. *Ferguson*."

45. Which option BEST describes what was sanctioned by the Supreme Court in the *Plessy v. Ferguson* case of 1896?

a. Segregation, or the idea of separate but equal treatment for African Americans
b. Integration and equal treatment for African Americans
c. Army regiments that had a majority of black servicemen
d. Army regiments that had only black servicemen

46. In the 1954 *Hernandez v. Texas* case, the Supreme Court decided that white and Hispanic could be considered different "classes" because of the way Hispanics had been unfairly treated in Texas. What was a MAIN effect of this decision?

a. Hispanics accused of crimes still faced juries composed only of white Americans
b. African Americans also started to be considered as a different class, instead of as a different race
c. Hispanics were now an identifiable minority group and their segregation could be prohibited under the *Brown* decision of 1954
d. Civil rights activists used the different class concept as their legal strategy for the next several decades, and the 14th Amendment was now applied to Hispanics as well as to African Americans

47. If a high school student wanted to wear an armband to protest the US military presence in Afghanistan, which Supreme Court decision could the student cite as allowing him or her to wear that armband into school (as long as the student did not disrupt classes)?

a. *Hazelwood School District v. Kuhlmeier*, 1988
b. *Bethel School District No. 403 v. Fraser*, 1986
c. *Tinker v. Des Moines*, 1969
d. *Doremus v. Board of Education of Borough of Hawthorne*, 1952

48. In 1937, President Franklin D. Roosevelt was accused by opponents of trying to "pack the court," and his plan for courts was defeated by the US Senate. What was Roosevelt's plan for the judicial branch at that time?

a. Roosevelt wanted only Democrats to be appointed to federal district courts
b. Roosevelt wanted only Democrats to be appointed as Supreme Court justices
c. Roosevelt wanted to raise the total number of Supreme Court justices from nine to 15
d. Roosevelt wanted to raise the total number of federal district court judges from 94 to 100

49. Which choice below BEST shows an example of how one can "lobby" a congressperson?

a. Voting for your congressperson during an election campaign
b. Voting for your congressperson's opponent during an election
c. Reading the email newsletters your congressperson sends to supporters
d. Writing a letter to your congressperson about an issue that is important to you

Question 50 pertains to the following excerpt from *The Black Experience in America*, author Norman Coombs describes a 1960s sit-in:

> "In a matter of weeks, student sit-ins were occurring at segregated lunch counters all across the South. College and high school students by the thousands joined the Civil Rights Movement. These students felt the need to form their own organization to mobilize and facilitate the spontaneous demonstrations which were springing up everywhere."

50. Student "sit-ins" are BEST described as which kind of way to participate in the democratic process?

a. Displaying Black Power to incite fear
b. Litigating
c. Lobbying
d. Non-violent protesting

51. In the PATRIOT Act first passed after September 11, 2001, the government could monitor religious and political institutions without suspecting criminal activity just in case it might assist a terror investigation. Which phrase BEST describes a constitutional right violated by such actions?

a. Right to legal representation
b. Right to a speedy and public trial
c. Right against involuntary servitude
d. Freedom of association or assembly

Use the excerpt and your knowledge of social studies to answer the following question:

Alexis de Tocqueville, in Democracy in America, wrote in 1840 about America

"The nearer the citizens are drawn to the common level of an equal and similar condition, the less prone does each man become to place implicit faith in a certain man or a certain class of men. But his readiness to believe the multitude increases, and opinion is more than ever mistress of the world. Not only is common opinion the only guide which private judgment retains amongst a democratic people, but amongst such a people it possesses a power infinitely beyond what it has elsewhere."

52. Which American traits was Alexis de Tocqueville describing in this excerpt?

a. Egalitarianism and populism
b. Individualism and liberty
c. Laissez-faire politics and individualism
d. Populism and liberty

53. The Sherman Antitrust Act of 1890 was the first federal law attempting to limit what kind of businesses?

a. Businesses that had monopolies or cartels
b. Businesses owned by foreigners
c. Companies that used child laborers
d. Companies that had lost the trust of their customers

54. What was an economic effect of the 1862 Homestead Act?

a. Agriculture became the top business in the US
b. The Homestead Act led to the formation of a "Farmers for the Economy" political group
c. Pioneers moved westward, built towns and schools, and created new states from former territories
d. The Act did not give enough incentives for people to move west, so the frontier did not get settled until much later in the 1800s

55. What was an economic effect of the Spanish-American War that could MOST likely be considered a positive economic benefit for the US?

a. Acquisition of island territories that could provide new markets
b. Chance to invest money in Spain and other foreign countries
c. Cost of rebuilding ships that had been damaged in the war
d. Cost of sending aid to poor people in Cuba

56. In war times, a government typically has three main ways to raise money to finance a war: borrowing from the public, printing money, and a third way. During World War I, the US government did not want to directly print money, as that might have driven down the gold standard. What was the third way to raise money for the war that was used in 1917?

a. Borrowing money from foreign governments
b. Cutting domestic government programs
c. Raising taxes, in the form of a War Revenue Act
d. Selling war bonds to the public

57. Speculation, which sometimes includes risky business transactions for a possible quick profit, was common regarding housing prices around 2003-2007, helping cause the current economic recession. What is one similarity between this fact and a cause of the 1929-1930s Great Depression?

a. Housing prices became too high in the 1930s, helping cause the Great Depression
b. Speculation on housing prices in the 1920s helped cause the Great Depression
c. Speculation in the 1920s stock market helped cause the Great Depression
d. A 1920s recession led to the Great Depression

58. World trade declined by 66 percent from 1929 to 1934, helping cause the Great Depression of 1929-1939. What form of US "protectionism" helped cause the decline in world trade?

a. Bank failures across the US
b. The monetary policy of the Federal Reserve System
c. The lowering of US tariffs on imported goods
d. The raising of US tariffs on imported goods

Use the graph and your knowledge of social studies to answer the following question:

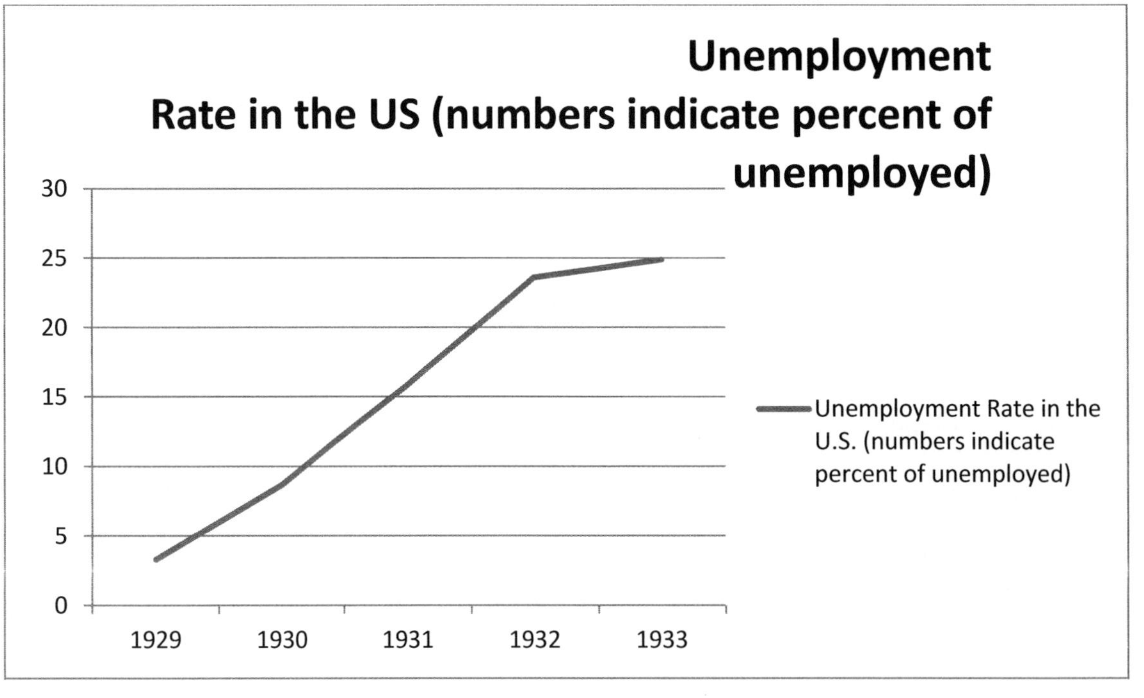

Statistics from the US Bureau of Labor

59. What is one conclusion that can be made based on this chart?

a. High US unemployment starting in 1929 helped cause the Great Depression
b. US unemployment was higher in the early 1930s than unemployment in other countries
c. High US unemployment showed a small decrease and then held steady in the early 1930s
d. The Great Depression caused a steep increase in the rate of unemployment in the US

60. From 1929-1939, the Mexican population in the US dropped by 40 percent. What was a main cause of this drop?

a. The Great Depression and lack of jobs led Mexican Americans to voluntarily leave the US
b. The Great Depression led to mass deportations of Mexican Americans by the US government
c. Many Mexican Americans had served in World War I and did not want to fight in future wars for the US
d. Mexican Americans were tiring of the racism and discrimination in the US and were voluntarily leaving the US

Use the list and your knowledge of social studies to answer the following question:

- During World War II, the US government put out the following list of information (paraphrased below) on why people should use less sugar in their kitchens:
- Soldiers need sugar, and overall military needs for sugar are high.
- The ships that usually bring sugar into the US are being used to bring supplies to battle fronts.
- There are currently not enough workers at sugar refineries and shipping ports due to the need for military service people.
- In summary, do not apply for more sugar than you really need!

61. What was the name and reason for this government program?

a. Food Safety Act, to ensure that food supplies were safe during the war
b. G.I. Bill, to ensure that servicemen got enough food and other supplies
c. New Deal, to ensure that poorer families would get enough food supplies during the war
d. Rationing, because important supplies, including food, were scarce and in high demand during the war

Use the list and your knowledge of social studies to answer the following question:

- US shipbuilding industry
- Los Alamos nuclear facility
- All-American Girls Professional Baseball League
- Washington D.C. government office jobs

62. Which choice BEST describes what the items on the above list have in common?

a. These were areas where women could find employment in non-traditional ways because of manpower shortage during World War I
b. These were areas where women could find employment in non-traditional ways because of manpower shortage during World War II
c. These were all organizations that received federal government funding in the 1930s
d. These were all organizations the received federal government funding in the 1940s

Use the excerpt and your knowledge of social studies to answer the following question:

In this excerpt from *The Black Experience in America*, author Norman Coombs describes 1941 negotiations between civil rights activist A. Philip Randolph, who was planning a March on Washington by African Americans, and President Franklin D. Roosevelt:

"Finally, Roosevelt contacted Randolph and offered to issue an executive order barring discrimination in defense industries and promised to put "teeth" in the order, provided Randolph call off the march. When Randolph became convinced that Roosevelt's intentions were sincere, he complied.

Roosevelt fulfilled his promise by issuing Executive Order 8802, which condemned discrimination on the grounds of race, color, or creed. Then, he established the Fair Employment Practices Commission and assigned to it the responsibility for enforcing the order."

63. What conclusion can BEST be made based on this excerpt?

a. Jobs for African Americans increased during World War II because of manpower needs and because of an anti-discrimination order from the president
b. Jobs for African Americans increased during World War II because of manpower needs alone, and the anti-discrimination order was probably not really needed
c. A. Philip Randolph was just bluffing about planning a March on Washington
d. President Franklin D. Roosevelt was not really worried about African Americans marching on Washington, but he gave in to Randolph's request for an Executive Order anyway

Use the "Cause and Effects" chart and your knowledge of social studies to answer the following question:

Cause: An important bill is passed in both Congress and the Senate and signed by President Franklin D. Roosevelt in 1944.

↓

Effect: Men with only high school educations could now go to college.

↓

Effect: Some of those men became doctors, lawyers, engineers, or joined other middle class professions.

↓

Effect: The middle class jobs and loans from the same bill allow men to buy houses.

↓

Effect: Entire suburbs are built with new homes for newly middle class families.

64. Complete this "Cause and Effects" chart by filling in a missing piece of information for "Cause." What was the name of the bill passed in 1944?

a. Executive Order 9981
b. G.I. Bill
c. Smith Act of 1944
d. Taft-Hartley Act

65. The 1950s included growing income and affluence, a larger middle class, and a baby boom. What other 1950s trend can BEST be considered an effect of those three factors?

a. Increased consumer spending and consumption
b. Military-industrial complex
c. Rock and roll music
d. The Cold War

66. The GATT (General Agreement on Tariffs and Trade) organization was started in 1947 by about 150 countries, including the US, to help regulate trade between them. What is the new name of the organization that GATT has now become, and is the US still a member?

a. International Trade Administration (ITA); yes, the US is still a member
b. International Trade Administration (ITA); no, the US is no longer a member
c. World Trade Organization (WTO), yes, the US is still a member
d. World Trade Organization (WTO); no, the US is no longer a member

67. The first laptop computers were produced in the early 1980s and the cost to buy one was over $1,000. What are some reasons that laptop computers cost less today?

a. The government has set price controls on products such as laptop computers that would be used in businesses
b. In the free enterprise system, many companies now produce laptop computers and compete to sell them at lower costs
c. The earliest laptop computers had a sales tax added to their cost that has since been removed by government legislation
d. Laptop computers today can perform better and they have more functionality and memory than the earliest laptop computers had

68. What advantages does the 20th century invention of electric cars contribute to improving the standard of living in the US (assuming that they are used)?

a. Electric cars go faster than gas-powered vehicles so they could improve efficiency, convenience, and productivity in the US
b. Electric cars have better creature comforts in their interiors than gas-powered cars, increasing the standard of living for Americans using such cars
c. Electric cars take less time to recharge than gas-powered cars take to re-fuel, thereby improving US efficiency, convenience, and productivity
d. Electric cars have no tailpipe emissions, helping the US have less air pollution; they lessen the US's dependence on foreign oil; and they are cheaper to operate than gas-powered cars, helping Americans save money

Answer Key and Explanations for Test #2

1. D: It gives the correct defining characteristic of the Roaring Twenties Era. The economy was strong with a great demand for new products, while culture in this era, also known as the "Jazz Age," became more experimental. A student might pick choice A, which defines the Cold War Era, if he or she focuses on the fact that it is also an era immediately following a World War. A student can rule out the other choices if they know how to correctly define the World War II and Great Depression Eras.

2. C: Jonathan Trumbull is the correct answer for which Founding Father was governor of Connecticut during and after the Revolutionary War. The other names are all of Founding Fathers, but none were governor of Connecticut. Rush, Witherspoon and Carroll all signed the Declaration of Independence; Carroll was a US Senator for Maryland while Rush lived in Pennsylvania and Witherspoon in New Jersey.

3. A: It shows the student's knowledge of the importance of 1914 events as a turning point for the start of World War I in Europe: "World War I had started; Germany had invaded other Belgian cities and was going to invade Antwerp also." The other choices are incorrect because Italy, Russia, and England were not invading Belgium.

4. D: It lists true contributions by John Jay to early. Choice A is partly correct about the first Chief Justice, but Jay was a Minister to Spain, not to France. Choice B correctly places him in New York, but he did not sign the Declaration or become mayor of New York City. Choice C has Minister of Spain correct, but Jay did not serve in George Washington's army during the war.

5. D: Ella Baker was a civil rights leader but born in 1903. Rosa Parks was part of the 1960s civil rights movement. Sojourner Truth lived near the time of Ida B. Wells, but she had died by 1883. Ida B. Wells is the correct answer, and she was known as a journalist, muckraker, reform leader, and fighter against lynchings.

6. D: While the photo shows World War I airplane warfare over England, it also took place over other countries like Germany and France, so choice A is incorrect. Airplane warfare first took place after the invention of the airplane, so during the Civil War could not be a correct choice. The American allies and the German side went back and forth in terms of airplane technology superiority, so choice B is not correct. Choice D is the MOST likely answer choice. Airplanes had their first warfare use during WWI, at first just for taking spy photographs, but were also used later in the war for firing guns and dropping bombs. The photo illustrates the fact that airplanes were in use during WWI for firing guns and dropping bombs.

7. A: Sanford B. Dole was the President of the Republic of Hawaii, and he did argue for annexation of Hawaii by the United States. Students familiar with the time period should know that he was not the President of the United States or the President of the US Senate. The excerpt may help them realize this fact. Also, Hawaii did not become a state officially until the 1950s, so choice B is incorrect.

8. B: The BEST summarizing title for the list is "How the Spanish-American War Helped the US Become a World Power." President Theodore Roosevelt did help the US become a world power, but that was after the events on the list (Spanish-American War events) because he was not president until 1901, after the war of 1898. Isolationism did give way to Imperialism in the 1890s, but it did not lead to or cause imperialism. The War of 1812 is an incorrect answer for students who know their historical dates and war events.

9. D: In point 14 of his 1918 speech Wilson was proposing a League of Nations which would eventually become the United Nations. If the student reads the excerpt carefully, and knows general history about the United Nations, the student will know that having the US involved in such a league would be a contrast to Wilson's pre-War policy of neutrality. The other choices given make references to phrases found in the excerpt, but they are not statements that contrast with a policy of neutrality and are incorrect answer choices.

10. A: The 16th Amendment is the correct answer for which amendment dealt with collecting income taxes to help fund progressive government goals. While all the amendments listed were championed by Progressive Era reformers, and all were around the same time period, the other amendments listed dealt with voting issues or prohibition, not with income taxes.

11. D: It is correct for why the Battle of the Argonne Forest was difficult and important. The illustration gives a clue to the answer because it shows a deep trench (though it also shows a forest, so the student also needs general social studies knowledge). The battle was difficult because the Germans were so entrenched in this forest, having built deep trenches there; and important because it was one of the final battles of the war and helped break through Germany's western front. The deeply forested nature of the area mentioned in choice C was also a difficulty, but that choice is incorrect because it claims the Germans won that battle when they did not. Some German soldiers were taken as prisoners of war during the battle, and there may have been some Allied prisoners, but that was not the purpose of the battle. There was air support provided to the Allies in that battle, so choice A is incorrect.

12. C: It is the BEST and only definition of the initiative process: It allowed citizens to introduce legislation proposals at a local or state level by gathering petitions, and proposals would then be addressed by lawmakers or placed on ballots for a vote. The other answer choices give definitions of "referendum" (choice A), "recall" (choice B), and also describe simply visiting a state legislature to give testimony about an issue (choice D), none of which define the "initiative" process.

13. B: "Nativism," a philosophy of the time period that native-born white Americans were superior to foreign born Americans, helped cause the Emergency Quota Act that limited immigrants in 1921. The other options were all social issues of the same time period, but not the main cause for limiting immigration. The Harlem Renaissance and Women's Suffrage Movement did not have such qualms with immigrants. Prohibition was partly caused by anti-immigrant sentiment such as against Germans after WWI, but Prohibition did not cause the Quota Act as much as Nativism.

14. C: It would BEST go next in the timeline's factual sequence of events because the other choices are not factually correct: thousands of Japanese-American men, women and children are relocated to internment camps. They were not forced to leave the US, and they were not forced to move from west coast to east coast (many internment camps were on the west coast). Japanese-American men did eventually start to be drafted for military service during World War II, and many did fight in that war for the US

15. D: It is the correct answer for this particular group of children, although choices A and B might be good guesses. There were German youth who wanted to avoid serving in Nazi armies, but they did not go into hiding in as great numbers as did Jewish youth trying to escape the Holocaust. There were children who awaited fake passports, but mostly to escape to the US or other safe countries, as Israel was not founded until after World War II. The correct answer is that "They were Jewish and had to be hidden from Nazis in order to survive the Holocaust, the attempted extermination of the Jewish population by Nazi Germany."

16. D: The Tuskegee Airmen was another name for the 332nd Fighter Group. The African-American men in the photo give the clue that it was the Tuskegee Airmen and not the Flying Tigers, who were Chinese American. The Tuskegee Airmen were an African-American group of fighter pilots in WWII, which should be general social studies knowledge at this grade level. Red Barons were in WWI, and Top Guns are navy pilots, nicknamed in a later time period than WWII.

17. A: NATO formed for the purpose of defending Europe from possible encroachment by communist Soviet Union armies which had invaded and were controlling some central and eastern European countries after WWII. Choice B and C may have eventually become other purposes for NATO in later years, but were not the original reasons for the formation of NATO. Choice D is incorrect because Germany did not immediately reunite after the war.

18. D: The Vietnam War was fought by the US in Vietnam because of the Domino Theory. China was the "first domino" in the theory, in that it became a communist nation before other Asian countries, but the US did not fight a war there. The US has also had shaky relations with Burma more recently, but did not fight a war there or in Thailand.

19. C: It is the correct result from the increased media coverage and availability. News with graphic images and interviews with frustrated soldiers resulted in a decrease of American public support for the war. It did not result in increased American support or in more men registering for the draft. The choice about Walter Cronkite could be a good guess, except that in 1970 Cronkite declared the war a "bloody stalemate," thus echoing and influencing the opinions of a majority of Americans about the Vietnam War.

20. A: Cesar Chavez, along with Dolores Huerta and Gilbert Padilla, helped start the NFWA in 1962. Students who know a little about Chavez and his lifelong activism for Hispanic migrant workers should be able to choose the correct answer. A student might incorrectly pick Hector P. Garcia or Felix Longoria for being others from the Mexican American civil rights movements (Garcia a doctor, and Longoria a WWII soldier). Or a student might pick Martin Luther King, Jr. because he also helped workers form unions, although not as much for farmers as for urban city workers.

21. B: The excerpt states that Johnson did want to carry on Kennedy's agenda and legacy, and that included in the field of Civil Rights, despite Johnson originally being a southerner. So the correct answer is B, Congress passed a Civil Rights Act in 1964 and President Johnson signed it. Students reading the excerpt carefully and having a good general knowledge of civil rights history should be able to make that correct prediction.

22. B: The Camp David Accords is the correct name for this historical event which included the 1979 leaders of Egypt and Israel making agreements with both the help and witnessing of US President Jimmy Carter. The Arab Spring is a more current event (2010-2011), and Peace through Strength was a Reagan-era philosophy. Palestinians are mentioned in the Camp David Accords, so choice C could be a good guess, but general social studies knowledge of the Middle East should help students remember that the PLO is Yasser Arafat's organization.

23. B: Malcolm X is the correct speaker of the excerpt's long quotation, as he is the only one on the list from the Black Power movement. James Sherman did a Freedom March and was murdered, which inspired some Black Power rallies, but he himself was not the advocate of a less peaceful movement. Martin Luther King, Jr. was the main advocate of nonviolent social change, so he would not have spoken the quote about "guerrilla tactics." William Clay was a representative and leader of the Black Caucus in Congress, not a revolutionary figure.

24. B: Jobs, land, and religious and political freedoms were all reasons why immigrants imagined that they would have better lives by coming to America in the late 1800s. Theodore Roosevelt was not president until 1901. Native Americans were not promised all of these things during that time period, or at least that would not be the BEST answer. Settlers did rush to California and the west for land, but not for the other items on that list, and gold is not on the list, which makes that choice a poor answer option.

25. C: The clue in the excerpt about American troops helping the stressed French and British troops should let the student know that the excerpt refers to World War I or World War II. If they read closely enough to see General Pershing's involvement, then they should know from general social studies knowledge at this grade level that Pershing was the commander of American Expeditionary Forces during World War I, and therefore C is the correct answer.

26. A: W.E.B. DuBois was a famous African American muckraking journalist for the NAACP's magazine in the early 1900s. Booker T. Washington was a contemporary of DuBois, but not a muckraking journalist. Gaines was a former slave who became a Texas State Senator, but Gaines died in 1900 and therefore could not be the correct answer. Marcus Garvey had a writing career advocating civil rights, but in a newspaper he started called *The Negro World*.

27. B: Students who know about the US Office of War Information should know that the purpose was to get out messages that would build morale and raise spirits. They also tried to recruit women for wartime work during WWII. They sometimes used famous stars such as Ethel Merman to further appeal to women. Their purpose was not to sell Broadway or movie tickets, nor was it to encourage women to stay at home.

28. C: The speech is from President Richard M. Nixon, who was about to become, in 1972, the first US president to visit the People's Republic of China. The other presidents listed are good guesses as they are from similar time periods and might have made similar speeches about China and the Soviet Union, but they are incorrect choices.

29. A: The Fall of Saigon happened in April 1975 and marked the end of the Vietnam War and the beginning of Vietnam's reunification under communist rule. A student might pick one of the other events because they were all events that did happen in the course of the Vietnam War, but they happened on earlier dates, not in April 1975, and were not the final event that marked the end of the war or South Vietnam's surrender.

30. C: The 26th Amendment is the youth voting rights amendment allowing 18-year-olds to vote, signed by President Nixon. The Vietnam War gave more urgency to the "old enough to fight, old enough to vote" slogan. The other amendment choices are in similar time frames and close enough to the 26th Amendment to possibly confuse a student who has not fully studied some of the more important amendments such as the 26th.

31. A: It is the BEST title for the list, The Causes of the 1935 Dust Bowl. The lack of ground cover was a cause of the Dust Bowl, but could also be considered a possible effect of dust storms also. But that is the only item on the list that would also be an effect of the Dust Bowl. The Sun Belt also had some years of drought, but the other items would not fit for Sun Belt as much, or for the Rust Belt except for possibly poor agricultural practices.

32. C: It is the BEST summary of the paragraph's main idea for settlers headed to the Great Plains in stage coach wagons: Fording the Platte River was thought to be dangerous, but turned out to mostly be time-consuming and a little inconvenient: time consuming because it "consumed" a whole day and inconvenient in that drivers and wagon boxes got wet. Choice A is incorrect because the wagon in the paragraph did not get caught in quicksand. Choice B is incorrect because it was not a quick and easy fording (it consumed a whole day). Choice D is a correct and true statement, but it has to do with a detail of the trip after the river crossing, and does not deal with the paragraph's main idea of describing the river crossing.

33. A: The most likely conclusion based on the US Census data chart is that rural to urban migration was a probable trend between the years 1890 and 1930. Both rural and urban areas grew in population numbers, making choices C and D incorrect, but urban areas grew by a much larger margin, meaning that there was probably migration from rural areas in addition to general population growth as a factor for the different numbers. Choice B is incorrect because urban to rural migration numbers are not shown on the chart.

34. D: Choice A is incorrect because Al Gore was not yet speaking on global warming issues during that time period. Choice B does not make sense in the context of the timeline because all the other events listed deal with environmental issues. Choice C confuses the establishment of the National Park System with the EPA. The park system was established earlier by Theodore Roosevelt, which should be part of the student's general social studies knowledge. Choice D is correct: Nixon established the EPA in December 1970.

35. D: It is the best reason why sustainable development is needed: The continued, forecasted population growth can damage the environment with greater stresses on oceans, food supplies, and land. Even though global warming (mentioned in choice C) is another reason why sustainable development is needed, the statement in choice C that population growth has stabilized is false. Fertility rates have fallen in some areas, but the world population will continue to expand for many years before possibly stabilizing. Choices A and B are not completely true statements and not good reasons for sustainable development.

36. D: A student picking answer D shows an understanding of a negative impact of the Beat Generation promoting the drug LSD: While some people may have felt that LSD was psychologically helpful, many people experienced bad effects such as fear or psychosis from the drug, and the drug was and still is illegal. The drug has been illegal since 1966, so choices A and B are incorrect. Choice C is also incorrect in that politicians were not the main people influenced by the Beat Generation to experiment with the drug.

37. B: Reading the excerpt and the proud quotes in it about Harlem should lead students to the correct answer about the impact of the Harlem Renaissance on African-American society in the 1920s: it gave African Americans a new sense of pride and confidence in their culture. It did not make them feel relegated to a "ghetto," as they chose to live in Harlem and made it a nice place to live. But blacks also lived in other cities, making choice C incorrect. Choice D is incorrect because the first part of the excerpt describes all kinds of people coming to participate in the Harlem Renaissance, not just artists, musicians, and writers, as might be popularly thought to be true.

38. A: It is the right choice for a generalization based on the bulleted list: American culture can spread globally through entertainment such as rap and hip-hop music, but that same culture sometimes gets reconstituted into new forms in other countries. Choice B is incorrect because rap and hip-hop have spread from the US to other countries also. Hollywood was not the main medium for spreading rap and hip-hop, since they are forms of music and not films, making choice C incorrect. Choice D is incorrect because rap and hip-hop mostly originated in the US

39. B: It best shows contributions of Italian-American women in the field of politics: The first woman to run for US Vice President was Geraldine Ferraro in 1984, and the first woman elected governor in her own right was Ella T. Grasso of Connecticut in 1975. The other choices show Italian-American women (or in one case a Latina woman, Sonia Sotomayor) making contributions in other fields that are not as political (education, Miss America, etc.). Some of the names listed are actually Italian-American men: Don DeLillo and Jerre Mangione.

40. B: Students with general social studies knowledge at this grade level will have heard of the Quaker religious group, who were active in the Abolitionist movement, women's rights movement, and pacifist/peace movements throughout US history, because all those movements agree with their religious views on equality and peace. The correct answer of B, the McCarthyism movement, is therefore an example of one movement that Quakers were NOT as involved in. In fact, Edward R. Murrow, one of the biggest opponents of McCarthy's "Un-American Activities Committee," was raised as a Quaker.

41. B: Eleanor Roosevelt was the First Lady who was also an honorary chair of the Red Cross. However, all of the First Ladies listed were First Ladies during war times, so they could be good guesses. But a student who knows the particular contributions of Eleanor Roosevelt to American politics and society should know the correct answer.

42. D: It best explains the fame and military burial honors for Mexican-American Roy Benavidez: He won a Congressional Medal of Honor and a Purple Heart for his brave military service and actions in the Vietnam War. He did serve in the Korean War briefly, but did not win his awards for that service. Choices A and B are false statements.

43. C: The freedom from unreasonable search and seizure was the constitutional right violated by the FBI when they searched the homes of Japanese Americans without search warrants during World War II. The other rights may have been violated in other ways by the government at the same time (also against Japanese Americans), but not in this particular given example. A student that understands the Constitution will answer correctly.

44. D: All Native Americans were granted US citizenship by the American Indian Citizenship Act of 1924. Having to take a citizenship test sounds correct, as many immigrants do that today, but it is not the correct answer. It is correct that some Native Americans achieved citizenship by marrying white citizens or by serving in the US military, but not all Native Americans became citizens until passage of the act in 1924.

45. A: A student reading the excerpt closely and knowing their general social studies history about *Plessy v. Ferguson* will choose the correct answer for what it decreed: segregation, or the idea of separate but equal treatment, for African Americans. A student might be fooled by the book title's "integration" mention to choose answer B. Or they may focus on the mention of black servicemen in the excerpt and incorrectly choose answers C or D. Choice D could describe an effect of *Plessy v. Ferguson*, but not the official thing being sanctioned. Choice A describes the sanction AND the effect of *Plessy v. Ferguson*.

46. D: Civil rights activists used the different "class," or "other white," concept as their legal strategy for the next several decades, and the 14th Amendment was now applied to Hispanics as well as to African Americans. This was the main effect of the *Hernandez v. Texas* decision. It did not have the effect described in choice C, as that happened in a 1970s Supreme Court case. Choice A was the problem being addressed in the Hernandez case, not an effect. And choice B has to do with African Americans, not Hispanics.

47. C: In 1969, *Tinker v. Des Moines* gave students the right to maintain their First Amendment right of free speech; in that case, wearing an armband to protest the Vietnam War, even inside of school buildings (as long as classes were not disrupted). The other cases also involve school districts and education, but were for different specific issues than this one. Although the Bethel and Kuhlmeier cases also touched on the First Amendment, in those cases it was in relation to school assemblies and school newspapers, not school attire.

48. C: President Roosevelt's plan for the judicial branch in 1937 was to raise the total number of Supreme Court justices from 9 to 15. His plan was defeated by the US Senate. The other answer choices sound like plausible ways that one might try to "pack the courts," but they are not correct answers for that time period, which students with a general history knowledge at this grade level should know.

49. D: Writing a letter to your congressperson about an issue that is important to you is the BEST example of how to "lobby" a congressperson. (Visiting, calling, or emailing are other lobbying methods.) Just reading the congressperson's email might be a first step, but not the best example of lobbying. Voting for the congressperson is also just a first step to get him or her into office, and not part of the actual lobbying campaign.

50. D: Student sit-ins were an example in the 1960s of non-violent protesting that took place mostly under the guidance and philosophy of Martin Luther King, Jr. These were not displays of Black Power to incite fear, although those also occurred separately in the 1960s under leaders such as Malcolm X. Sit-ins were not a form of lobbying or litigation, although those are also non-violent in their nature.

51. D: Out of the four choices offered, the freedom of association or assembly BEST describes what constitutional right would be violated by the monitoring of religious or political groups, because people should be free to assemble and associate with whoever they wish without fear of government intervention. The other rights listed may have also been violated by the PATRIOT Act, but not in this particular example.

52. A: In this excerpt, de Tocqueville was discussing the American traits of egalitarianism ("citizens are drawn to the common level of an equal") and populism, or the interests and belief of the popular opinion ("common opinion" is powerful). The other choices all mention traits discussed by de Tocqueville in other parts of his book, but not in this particular excerpt.

53. A: The Sherman Antitrust Act of 1890 was the first law attempting to limit businesses that had monopolies. A student who understands that "trust" in this sense means a group of companies, and has come to mean "monopoly," may get the correct answer rather than choosing answer D, which uses a different meaning for the word "trust." It was not an attempt to limit businesses that were owned by foreigners or using child labor.

54. C: It is the best answer for the economic impact of the Homestead Act: Pioneers moved westward, built towns and schools, and created new states from former territories. The Act did cause a lot of westward settlement, unlike answer choice D, but it did not make agriculture the number one business in America, and it did not result in a political group called "Farmers for the Economy," even though those sound like answer choices that would be telling an economic impact of a law.

55. A: Although giving aid to poor people in Cuba does confer moral benefits for the donating country, making an argument for choice D, choice A is the BEST choice for the economic benefit to the US of the Spanish-American War: the acquisition of island territories (such as Puerto Rico and the Philippines) that could provide new markets. Investing in Spain and the cost of repairing damaged ships would be economic negative costs of the war.

56. C: Raising taxes in the form of a War Revenue Act is the correct answer for this specific question of what was a third way to raise money that was used in 1917. The government may have cut some domestic spending, but not specifically in 1917 for this war. War bonds were sold to the public, but that is a method of borrowing money from the public, which was already mentioned as the first possible way to raise money for war. Choice A was not used in World War I; other governments did make purchases from the US to help the war cause.

57. C: Speculation in the 1920s stock market helped cause the Great Depression. This is similar to speculation on the housing market in the 2000s causing today's recession, showing the student's mastery of skills in comparing and contrasting. Speculation on housing, high housing prices, and a 1920s recession were not causes of the Great Depression. The 1920s was a period of prosperity, not recession.

58. D: The kind of protectionism act by the US that helped lead to a decline in worldwide trade, thus contributing to the Great Depression, was the raising of US tariffs on imported goods. This led to other countries retaliating by raising tariffs also, so US imports and exports were affected. Choice A and B were other causes of the Great Depression, but not causes of the decline in worldwide trade directly. Choice C is the opposite of the correct answer.

59. D: A student will show that he or she can read a graph correctly and understand general social studies knowledge about the effects of the Great Depression if they choose D, "The Great Depression caused a steep increase in the rate of unemployment in the US" The rate was not originally high in 1929, but did steadily increase in the years following 1929. A student may think the graph shows the rate "steady" at one point, but it is still going up between 1932 and 1933. The unemployment rate of other countries is not shown on the graph, therefore making choice B incorrect.

60. B: While choices A and D may be partly responsible for some Mexican Americans leaving the US, several hundred thousand Mexican Americans were forcibly deported by the US government (using troops to force them over the border) because of the Great Depression and lack of jobs in the US So choice B is the correct answer as the main cause of the drop in the US-Mexican population in the 1930s. Choice C was not really a factor in the drop.

61. D: "Rationing" was the name for this particular government program, and the reason for it was because food and other supplies were scarce and in greater demand during wartime. The G.I. Bill, Food Safety Act, and New Deal were all different kinds of government programs, some dealing with food but not all of them.

62. B: It best describes what all of the items on the list have in common. These were areas where women could find employment in non-traditional ways because of a manpower shortage during World War II. Women also worked outside the home in WWI, but Los Alamos and the baseball league were not set up that early. Choice D would be a good guess, but the All-American Girls Professional Baseball League was funded in the 1940s by businesses and businessmen, not by the federal government, unlike the other items on the list.

63. A: It is the best conclusion to be made based on the facts in the excerpt: Jobs for African Americans increased during World War II because of manpower needs and because of an anti-discrimination order from the president. The jobs would not have come without the executive order because there was still a lot of discrimination against African Americans in the 1940s (as is described in Coombs' book, paragraphs just before and after this excerpt). Roosevelt was concerned about Randolph planning a march because of how it might appear to US enemies during the war, and Randolph was not bluffing. Randolph said discrimination by whites, not his march, was the reason that the US would appear in a poor light to enemies or other countries.

64. B: The G.I. Bill, or Servicemen's Readjustment Act of 1944, was the name of the bill that had the myriad effects listed in the chart. The Taft-Hartley Act was an anti-labor bill under Truman; the Smith Act was a war time bill under FDR in 1940; and the Executive Order listed was one signed by Truman (although it would be a good guess because FDR did sign many "Executive Orders"). All the distracters are also near the same time period as the GI Bill, but students with a good general knowledge of history should get the correct answer.

65. A: Increased consumer spending and consumption can BEST be linked to the other three trends of the 1950s. An argument could be made that rock and roll music was also an effect, but that cannot be tied directly to other three factors listed in the question, and it is a more specific and less general answer and therefore less correct answer for being in a cause/effect relationship with the other general trends. The military-industrial complex and Cold War were other trends in the 1950s, but they were not tied to the three trends mentioned in the question.

66. C: The GATT is now named the World Trade Organization, or WTO, and the US is still a member. The student should know this from general social studies knowledge. If not, they might be able to rule out the ITA as a correct answer because "Administration" in the title gives a clue that the ITA is one country's (America's) internal organization, and not a worldwide organization.

67. B: The reason why laptop computers cost less today than in the early 1980s is that, because of the free enterprise system of the US, many companies now produce laptop computers and compete to sell them at lower costs. The government did not set price controls or take away any sales tax. Sales taxes vary from state to state. Choice D may be a true statement about how laptops have improved, but that option does not explain why the cost is less, and could even be used for an opposite argument for why laptops cost more to produce in modern times.

68. D: Statements A, B, and C all contain false statements about electric cars. Even if the student does not know enough about electric cars to determine that those statements are false, they probably would know enough to realize that statement D contains the best description of electric car advantages which contribute to a better standard of living for Americans using such cars: Electric cars have no tailpipe emissions, thus reducing air pollution in the US; they lessen the country's dependence on foreign oil; and they are cheaper to operate than gas-powered cars.

How to Overcome Test Anxiety

Just the thought of taking a test is enough to make most people a little nervous. A test is an important event that can have a long-term impact on your future, so it's important to take it seriously and it's natural to feel anxious about performing well. But just because anxiety is normal, that doesn't mean that it's helpful in test taking, or that you should simply accept it as part of your life. Anxiety can have a variety of effects. These effects can be mild, like making you feel slightly nervous, or severe, like blocking your ability to focus or remember even a simple detail.

If you experience test anxiety—whether severe or mild—it's important to know how to beat it. To discover this, first you need to understand what causes test anxiety.

Causes of Test Anxiety

While we often think of anxiety as an uncontrollable emotional state, it can actually be caused by simple, practical things. One of the most common causes of test anxiety is that a person does not feel adequately prepared for their test. This feeling can be the result of many different issues such as poor study habits or lack of organization, but the most common culprit is time management. Starting to study too late, failing to organize your study time to cover all of the material, or being distracted while you study will mean that you're not well prepared for the test. This may lead to cramming the night before, which will cause you to be physically and mentally exhausted for the test. Poor time management also contributes to feelings of stress, fear, and hopelessness as you realize you are not well prepared but don't know what to do about it.

Other times, test anxiety is not related to your preparation for the test but comes from unresolved fear. This may be a past failure on a test, or poor performance on tests in general. It may come from comparing yourself to others who seem to be performing better or from the stress of living up to expectations. Anxiety may be driven by fears of the future—how failure on this test would affect your educational and career goals. These fears are often completely irrational, but they can still negatively impact your test performance.

Elements of Test Anxiety

As mentioned earlier, test anxiety is considered to be an emotional state, but it has physical and mental components as well. Sometimes you may not even realize that you are suffering from test anxiety until you notice the physical symptoms. These can include trembling hands, rapid heartbeat, sweating, nausea, and tense muscles. Extreme anxiety may lead to fainting or vomiting. Obviously, any of these symptoms can have a negative impact on testing. It is important to recognize them as soon as they begin to occur so that you can address the problem before it damages your performance.

The mental components of test anxiety include trouble focusing and inability to remember learned information. During a test, your mind is on high alert, which can help you recall information and stay focused for an extended period of time. However, anxiety interferes with your mind's natural processes, causing you to blank out, even on the questions you know well. The strain of testing during anxiety makes it difficult to stay focused, especially on a test that may take several hours. Extreme anxiety can take a huge mental toll, making it difficult not only to recall test information but even to understand the test questions or pull your thoughts together.

Effects of Test Anxiety

Test anxiety is like a disease—if left untreated, it will get progressively worse. Anxiety leads to poor performance, and this reinforces the feelings of fear and failure, which in turn lead to poor performances on subsequent tests. It can grow from a mild nervousness to a crippling condition. If allowed to progress, test anxiety can have a big impact on your schooling, and consequently on your future.

Test anxiety can spread to other parts of your life. Anxiety on tests can become anxiety in any stressful situation, and blanking on a test can turn into panicking in a job situation. But fortunately, you don't have to let anxiety rule your testing and determine your grades. There are a number of relatively simple steps you can take to move past anxiety and function normally on a test and in the rest of life.

Physical Steps for Beating Test Anxiety

While test anxiety is a serious problem, the good news is that it can be overcome. It doesn't have to control your ability to think and remember information. While it may take time, you can begin taking steps today to beat anxiety.

Just as your first hint that you may be struggling with anxiety comes from the physical symptoms, the first step to treating it is also physical. Rest is crucial for having a clear, strong mind. If you are tired, it is much easier to give in to anxiety. But if you establish good sleep habits, your body and mind will be ready to perform optimally, without the strain of exhaustion. Additionally, sleeping well helps you to retain information better, so you're more likely to recall the answers when you see the test questions.

Getting good sleep means more than going to bed on time. It's important to allow your brain time to relax. Take study breaks from time to time so it doesn't get overworked, and don't study right before bed. Take time to rest your mind before trying to rest your body, or you may find it difficult to fall asleep.

Along with sleep, other aspects of physical health are important in preparing for a test. Good nutrition is vital for good brain function. Sugary foods and drinks may give a burst of energy but this burst is followed by a crash, both physically and emotionally. Instead, fuel your body with protein and vitamin-rich foods.

Also, drink plenty of water. Dehydration can lead to headaches and exhaustion, especially if your brain is already under stress from the rigors of the test. Particularly if your test is a long one, drink water during the breaks. And if possible, take an energy-boosting snack to eat between sections.

Along with sleep and diet, a third important part of physical health is exercise. Maintaining a steady workout schedule is helpful, but even taking 5-minute study breaks to walk can help get your blood pumping faster and clear your head. Exercise also releases endorphins, which contribute to a positive feeling and can help combat test anxiety.

When you nurture your physical health, you are also contributing to your mental health. If your body is healthy, your mind is much more likely to be healthy as well. So take time to rest, nourish your body with healthy food and water, and get moving as much as possible. Taking these physical steps will make you stronger and more able to take the mental steps necessary to overcome test anxiety.

Mental Steps for Beating Test Anxiety

Working on the mental side of test anxiety can be more challenging, but as with the physical side, there are clear steps you can take to overcome it. As mentioned earlier, test anxiety often stems from lack of preparation, so the obvious solution is to prepare for the test. Effective studying may be the most important weapon you have for beating test anxiety, but you can and should employ several other mental tools to combat fear.

First, boost your confidence by reminding yourself of past success—tests or projects that you aced. If you're putting as much effort into preparing for this test as you did for those, there's no reason you should expect to fail here. Work hard to prepare; then trust your preparation.

Second, surround yourself with encouraging people. It can be helpful to find a study group, but be sure that the people you're around will encourage a positive attitude. If you spend time with others who are anxious or cynical, this will only contribute to your own anxiety. Look for others who are motivated to study hard from a desire to succeed, not from a fear of failure.

Third, reward yourself. A test is physically and mentally tiring, even without anxiety, and it can be helpful to have something to look forward to. Plan an activity following the test, regardless of the outcome, such as going to a movie or getting ice cream.

When you are taking the test, if you find yourself beginning to feel anxious, remind yourself that you know the material. Visualize successfully completing the test. Then take a few deep, relaxing breaths and return to it. Work through the questions carefully but with confidence, knowing that you are capable of succeeding.

Developing a healthy mental approach to test taking will also aid in other areas of life. Test anxiety affects more than just the actual test—it can be damaging to your mental health and even contribute to depression. It's important to beat test anxiety before it becomes a problem for more than testing.

Study Strategy

Being prepared for the test is necessary to combat anxiety, but what does being prepared look like? You may study for hours on end and still not feel prepared. What you need is a strategy for test prep. The next few pages outline our recommended steps to help you plan out and conquer the challenge of preparation.

Step 1: Scope Out the Test

Learn everything you can about the format (multiple choice, essay, etc.) and what will be on the test. Gather any study materials, course outlines, or sample exams that may be available. Not only will this help you to prepare, but knowing what to expect can help to alleviate test anxiety.

Step 2: Map Out the Material

Look through the textbook or study guide and make note of how many chapters or sections it has. Then divide these over the time you have. For example, if a book has 15 chapters and you have five days to study, you need to cover three chapters each day. Even better, if you have the time, leave an extra day at the end for overall review after you have gone through the material in depth.

If time is limited, you may need to prioritize the material. Look through it and make note of which sections you think you already have a good grasp on, and which need review. While you are studying, skim quickly through the familiar sections and take more time on the challenging parts.

Write out your plan so you don't get lost as you go. Having a written plan also helps you feel more in control of the study, so anxiety is less likely to arise from feeling overwhelmed at the amount to cover.

Step 3: Gather Your Tools

Decide what study method works best for you. Do you prefer to highlight in the book as you study and then go back over the highlighted portions? Or do you type out notes of the important information? Or is it helpful to make flashcards that you can carry with you? Assemble the pens, index cards, highlighters, post-it notes, and any other materials you may need so you won't be distracted by getting up to find things while you study.

If you're having a hard time retaining the information or organizing your notes, experiment with different methods. For example, try color-coding by subject with colored pens, highlighters, or post-it notes. If you learn better by hearing, try recording yourself reading your notes so you can listen while in the car, working out, or simply sitting at your desk. Ask a friend to quiz you from your flashcards, or try teaching someone the material to solidify it in your mind.

Step 4: Create Your Environment

It's important to avoid distractions while you study. This includes both the obvious distractions like visitors and the subtle distractions like an uncomfortable chair (or a too-comfortable couch that makes you want to fall asleep). Set up the best study environment possible: good lighting and a comfortable work area. If background music helps you focus, you may want to turn it on, but otherwise keep the room quiet. If you are using a computer to take notes, be sure you don't have any other windows open, especially applications like social media, games, or anything else that could distract you. Silence your phone and turn off notifications. Be sure to keep water close by so you stay hydrated while you study (but avoid unhealthy drinks and snacks).

Also, take into account the best time of day to study. Are you freshest first thing in the morning? Try to set aside some time then to work through the material. Is your mind clearer in the afternoon or evening? Schedule your study session then. Another method is to study at the same time of day that you will take the test, so that your brain gets used to working on the material at that time and will be ready to focus at test time.

Step 5: Study!

Once you have done all the study preparation, it's time to settle into the actual studying. Sit down, take a few moments to settle your mind so you can focus, and begin to follow your study plan. Don't give in to distractions or let yourself procrastinate. This is your time to prepare so you'll be ready to fearlessly approach the test. Make the most of the time and stay focused.

Of course, you don't want to burn out. If you study too long you may find that you're not retaining the information very well. Take regular study breaks. For example, taking five minutes out of every hour to walk briskly, breathing deeply and swinging your arms, can help your mind stay fresh.

As you get to the end of each chapter or section, it's a good idea to do a quick review. Remind yourself of what you learned and work on any difficult parts. When you feel that you've mastered the material, move on to the next part. At the end of your study session, briefly skim through your notes again.

But while review is helpful, cramming last minute is NOT. If at all possible, work ahead so that you won't need to fit all your study into the last day. Cramming overloads your brain with more information than it can process and retain, and your tired mind may struggle to recall even previously learned information when it is overwhelmed with last-minute study. Also, the urgent nature of cramming and the stress placed on your brain contribute to anxiety. You'll be more likely to go to the test feeling unprepared and having trouble thinking clearly.

So don't cram, and don't stay up late before the test, even just to review your notes at a leisurely pace. Your brain needs rest more than it needs to go over the information again. In fact, plan to finish your studies by noon or early afternoon the day before the test. Give your brain the rest of the day to relax or focus on other things, and get a good night's sleep. Then you will be fresh for the test and better able to recall what you've studied.

Step 6: Take a Practice Test

Many courses offer sample tests, either online or in the study materials. This is an excellent resource to check whether you have mastered the material, as well as to prepare for the test format and environment.

Check the test format ahead of time: the number of questions, the type (multiple choice, free response, etc.), and the time limit. Then create a plan for working through them. For example, if you have 30 minutes to take a 60-question test, your limit is 30 seconds per question. Spend less time on the questions you know well so that you can take more time on the difficult ones.

If you have time to take several practice tests, take the first one open book, with no time limit. Work through the questions at your own pace and make sure you fully understand them. Gradually work up to taking a test under test conditions: sit at a desk with all study materials put away and set a timer. Pace yourself to make sure you finish the test with time to spare and go back to check your answers if you have time.

After each test, check your answers. On the questions you missed, be sure you understand why you missed them. Did you misread the question (tests can use tricky wording)? Did you forget the information? Or was it something you hadn't learned? Go back and study any shaky areas that the practice tests reveal.

Taking these tests not only helps with your grade, but also aids in combating test anxiety. If you're already used to the test conditions, you're less likely to worry about it, and working through tests until you're scoring well gives you a confidence boost. Go through the practice tests until you feel comfortable, and then you can go into the test knowing that you're ready for it.

Test Tips

On test day, you should be confident, knowing that you've prepared well and are ready to answer the questions. But aside from preparation, there are several test day strategies you can employ to maximize your performance.

First, as stated before, get a good night's sleep the night before the test (and for several nights before that, if possible). Go into the test with a fresh, alert mind rather than staying up late to study.

Try not to change too much about your normal routine on the day of the test. It's important to eat a nutritious breakfast, but if you normally don't eat breakfast at all, consider eating just a protein bar. If you're a coffee drinker, go ahead and have your normal coffee. Just make sure you time it so that the caffeine doesn't wear off right in the middle of your test. Avoid sugary beverages, and drink enough water to stay hydrated but not so much that you need a restroom break 10 minutes into the test. If your test isn't first thing in the morning, consider going for a walk or doing a light workout before the test to get your blood flowing.

Allow yourself enough time to get ready, and leave for the test with plenty of time to spare so you won't have the anxiety of scrambling to arrive in time. Another reason to be early is to select a good seat. It's helpful to sit away from doors and windows, which can be distracting. Find a good seat, get out your supplies, and settle your mind before the test begins.

When the test begins, start by going over the instructions carefully, even if you already know what to expect. Make sure you avoid any careless mistakes by following the directions.

Then begin working through the questions, pacing yourself as you've practiced. If you're not sure on an answer, don't spend too much time on it, and don't let it shake your confidence. Either skip it and come back later, or eliminate as many wrong answers as possible and guess among the remaining ones. Don't dwell on these questions as you continue—put them out of your mind and focus on what lies ahead.

Be sure to read all of the answer choices, even if you're sure the first one is the right answer. Sometimes you'll find a better one if you keep reading. But don't second-guess yourself if you do immediately know the answer. Your gut instinct is usually right. Don't let test anxiety rob you of the information you know.

If you have time at the end of the test (and if the test format allows), go back and review your answers. Be cautious about changing any, since your first instinct tends to be correct, but make sure you didn't misread any of the questions or accidentally mark the wrong answer choice. Look over any you skipped and make an educated guess.

At the end, leave the test feeling confident. You've done your best, so don't waste time worrying about your performance or wishing you could change anything. Instead, celebrate the successful completion of this test. And finally, use this test to learn how to deal with anxiety even better next time.

Review Video: Test Anxiety
Visit mometrix.com/academy and enter code: 100340

Important Qualification

Not all anxiety is created equal. If your test anxiety is causing major issues in your life beyond the classroom or testing center, or if you are experiencing troubling physical symptoms related to your anxiety, it may be a sign of a serious physiological or psychological condition. If this sounds like your situation, we strongly encourage you to seek professional help.

Online Resources

Due to our efforts to try to keep this book to a manageable length, we've created a link that will give you access to all of your online resources:

mometrix.com/resources719/sslaushistory

It's Your Moment, Let's Celebrate It!

Share your story @mometrixtestpreparation